PRAISE FOR
THE CREATIVE CTO

"Jim has done the industry a huge favor with a blueprint informed by his tremendous experience as a CTO. Till now, CTOs have been all over the map in terms of how they defined the role. This will be a welcome text for those aspiring to this key enterprise position."

—FRANK SLOOTMAN, FORMER CEO OF SNOWFLAKE, SERVICENOW, AND DATA DOMAIN, BOARD DIRECTOR, AND BESTSELLING AUTHOR

"*The Creative CTO* is a wonderful resource that not only sheds light on the CTO's role but also offers invaluable lessons on leadership and communication. Beyond technology, the book's emphasis on clear communication, fostering innovation, and maintaining focus will resonate deeply with any C-level leader."

—CHARLIE KAWWAS, PhD, PRESIDENT OF SEMICONDUCTOR SOLUTIONS GROUP AT BROADCOM

"Jim Adams was the most unique technologist I have ever worked with. He has always blended a true passion for technology, creativeness, hands-on delivery, pragmatism, and an inspirational style that brings teams along on the journey. Jim has captured 'the full monty' of attributes for a successful CTO as clearly as I have seen documented."

—MIKE GRIMALDI, CTO OF BALYASNY ASSET MANAGEMENT AND FORMER INVESTMENT BANKING CIO

www.amplifypublishinggroup.com

The Creative CTO: Intuitive Technology Leadership for the Modern Enterprise

©2025 James Boyd Adams. All Rights Reserved. No part of this publication may be reproduced, stored in a retrieval system or transmitted in any form by any means electronic, mechanical, or photocopying, recording or otherwise without the permission of the author.

For more information, please contact:
Amplify Publishing, an imprint of Amplify Publishing Group
620 Herndon Parkway, Suite 220
Herndon, VA 20170
info@amplifypublishing.com

Library of Congress Control Number: 2025900018

CPSIA Code: PRV0525A

ISBN-13: 979-8-89138-452-1

Printed in the United States

To Ellithia—from the moment that you were born, you have shown me what really mattered.

JAMES BOYD ADAMS

THE
CREATIVE
CTO

**INTUITIVE
TECHNOLOGY LEADERSHIP
for the
MODERN ENTERPRISE**

CONTENTS

FOREWORD ix
INTRODUCTION xi
Chapter 1: What Exactly Is a CTO? 1

PART I: ARCHITECTURE

Chapter 2: Defining Architecture 13
Chapter 3: Business Architecture 25
Chapter 4: Information Architecture 47
Chapter 5: Application Architecture 61
Chapter 6: Technology Architecture 71
Chapter 7: Security Architecture 81

PART II: GOVERNANCE

Chapter 8: Architecture Governance 97
Chapter 9: "Just Enough" Oversight 127

PART III: STRATEGY

Chapter 10: Defining Strategy 139
Chapter 11: The Target Operating Model 161
Chapter 12: Managing Risk 181

PART IV: LEADERSHIP

Chapter 13: Being a Leader, Not a Manager 209
Chapter 14: Communication 223
Chapter 15: Last Words 231

ACKNOWLEDGMENTS 235
REFERENCES 237
ABOUT THE AUTHOR 241

FOREWORD

When I first met Jim Adams, I was struck by his rare combination of technical brilliance and practical leadership. He literally drew an architecture on a restaurant napkin as a starting point for our journey, and before we even began working together, he sent me a paper proposing how to structure the office of the CTO for maximum impact. Over the years, I've watched Jim navigate the complexities of global technology leadership with a creative yet disciplined approach that few can match. In *The Creative CTO*, he opens the door to his world, sharing hard-earned lessons from his career at some of the largest financial institutions on the planet. His journey—from writing BASIC code on a Sinclair ZX81 to shaping technology strategy at industry giants—is a testament to resilience, curiosity, and relentless self-improvement.

This book goes beyond theory, offering practical frameworks and strategies honed through real-world challenges at the highest levels of the industry. He blends technology expertise with executive insight, demystifying the CTO's role with a balance of technical precision and practical advice. His four pillars—Architecture, Governance, Strategy, and Leadership—are the tools he has wielded to solve some of the toughest problems in the industry. This book is not just a road map for aspiring CTOs but a playbook for any technology professional aiming to scale the heights of enterprise leadership. If you're serious about leading in today's technology-driven world, learning from Jim through *The Creative CTO* is not just an opportunity—it's a game changer.

**—MICHAEL WHITAKER, GLOBAL CIO AND MEMBER OF
THE EXECUTIVE COMMITTEE AT CANTOR FITZGERALD**

INTRODUCTION

Great leaders are almost always great simplifiers who can cut through argument, debate, and doubt to offer a solution everybody can understand.

—GEN. COLIN POWELL

As I moved from being a "real" code-creating technologist to a technology manager, technology leader, and ultimately a chief technology officer (CTO), I was sure that this was not only a well-traveled path but also one that must have been well documented. Surely others before me had not only made the same journey but had also thoroughly chronicled its many twists and turns.

However, having now been a CTO at some of the largest financial institutions in the world, I realized that the numerous articles and books I read on this journey had not prepared me for the reality of being in the role. Sure, they conveyed the broad expectations—be the "executive in charge of an organization's technological needs"[1] and "make decisions for the overarching technology infrastructure that closely align with the organization's goals"[2] —but nothing adequately prepared me for what the job truly entailed. Fewer still provided approaches that were both actionable and helpful.

My own journey into becoming a CTO was somewhat untraditional. I started programming in the early 1980s when my dad, an electrical engineer, bought my brother and me a Sinclair ZX81, for which he quickly doubled the memory from 1K to an impressive 2K! I soon became familiar with creating simple BASIC programs. Then in 1983 I was fortunate to be upgraded to a Sinclair Spectrum 48K, at the time a huge increase in capabilities. While studying for my Computer Science O-level, I became sufficiently proficient in BASIC to create a rudimentary *Pac-Man* game, complete with multiple screens and music transposed into "BEEP" commands. I've hung onto the thermal printout to this day (and I'm sure that only a few of you will know what this is!).

Then for a time, I didn't do much more with technology. In fact, I didn't do much more of *anything* academically and left school without the necessary A levels to go to university, as in the UK, you needed at least more than none. So I drifted into the job market, working in bars and retail stores, before becoming a data entry clerk for the Provident Mutual Life Assurance Association, then affectionately known by us all as "the Prov."

This ended up being my "big break." As an equal employment opportunity, the Prov allowed existing employees to take an aptitude test, which, if passed, would grant them admission to the graduate intake program in the technology department. With much encouragement from my dad—"You need to get a real job at some point, son!"—and some remonstrations from my then senior manager—"You really should just go to university!"—I signed up and passed with a score of 92 percent. At the tender age of nineteen, I secured my first paying programming job.

Even then I realized how fortunate I had been to secure the position. At the same time, I was also convinced that my lack of a computer science degree put me at a significant disadvantage to my peers. This set me on a path of self-improvement, research, and study as I endeavored to catch up. I bought numerous technology books, read all the manuals at work I could find, and enrolled in a set of Open University classes on Computing for Commerce and Industry. I was fortunate to establish good habits early on. The rigorous program of research and study I originally started to overcome my sense of impostor syndrome continues to this day.

My career progressed from mainframe to client-server, to the then-emerging relational database technologies, to the advent of Java and the internet. With each role, I often moved from purely technical leadership roles to ones that required more customer, project, or people management. When this happened, my engagement in technical activities would diminish. This served as a catalyst for changing roles or even firms, each time striving to remain technically focused. Yet after each move, I would invariably end up moving *away* from purely technical roles to having to display competence in these management responsibilities. Though I didn't realize it at the time, I was honing a variety of skills that I would ultimately need as a CTO.

One role in particular that I look back on and cherish for how it prepared me for later in life was working as a "custom development" engineer for the Oracle Corporation. This was in the mid-1990s, at the advent of the internet, an exciting time to be a technologist. My role involved helping companies adopt these emerging technologies. Oracle placed great importance on ensuring individuals focused on the necessary "soft skills" required to be successful when working on a client site, such as presentation, project management, and client relationship skills. I embraced these opportunities and had a marvelous time working on a number of projects: an early version of internet banking for the Bank of Ireland, an exhibit inventory systems for the Victoria and Albert Museum, cable TV video-on-demand solutions, and many more.

The variety of technical challenges and company cultures I was exposed to and had to operate in prepared me for my first financial services role at Goldman Sachs, another company that at the time also placed great importance on hiring well-rounded, comprehensive technologists. Goldman Sachs introduced me to financial services *and* senior leadership roles, including my first opportunity to be a CTO.

Over the next twenty years or so, I honed my understanding of the CTO role and the many broader responsibilities of a technology leader. I started as a wholesale banking business line CTO, first at Deutsche Bank and subsequently at J.P. Morgan, and finally became the group CTO and head of technology infrastructure at Citigroup.

In the process I found that the CTO role varies significantly from firm to firm. Some predominantly large, traditional institutions, such as those in financial services, tend to appoint a chief information officer (CIO) as the primary executive responsible for overseeing technology operations. Often these firms may not have a CTO at all. Sometimes the CTO is subordinate to the CIO, with responsibilities for technology governance and engineering practices only, leaving technology *strategy* to the CIO.

At other companies, principally "digital first" or technology firms, there is no CIO, only a CTO who has overall responsibilities for all technology activities. I have also experienced the situation where the CTO was a *peer* of the CIO, responsible for technology governance and engineering practices *and* responsible for the technology infrastructure and platforms that the CIOs had to leverage.

These organizational structures can be effective and impactful, with the positioning of the role aligning with the needs of the organization. I strongly believe that the CTO should always have *some* delivery responsibility in addition to oversight of governance and engineering practices, as without a grounded expectation to "eat your own dog food,"[3] there is always a risk that the processes introduced are less than optimal. This is a personal preference, but it is one born of experience. In all cases there is consistency in the core responsibilities of the role.

As the senior executive focused on an organization's technical requirements and strategy, a CTO really must span several areas of responsibility. They must articulate the appropriate approach for the development and operations of technology. They must create technology policies and standards that ensure effective risk management. They must confirm compliance with the legal or regulatory considerations in their industry or region. And as you'll see, the list goes on.

For the financial services industry, which is highly regulated and often subject to regulatory reviews, it's critical to set appropriate standards that can be demonstrated in execution and connected to risk management. These must cover both the adoption of architectural methodology and development standards—design, coding, testing, and release—that all technology products require.

It took me some time to appreciate the importance of an appropriate level of detail and prescription within the standards. By that, I mean ensuring that suitable controls were introduced and sufficient evidence of adherence was recorded to ensure the right level of risk management. At the same time, these standards should not become so burdensome and bureaucratic that they impeded the development process. Likewise, insufficient standards, while allowing development to proceed with less friction, ultimately increased the risk of critical failures or regulatory jeopardy, all of which would require additional investments to remediate.

After over a decade or more as a corporate CTO, I have had the great pleasure of working in many prestigious organizations. More importantly, I have had the opportunity to work with some of the brightest and best in the technology industry. Over many diverse collaborations, I have gradually developed a comprehensive understanding of the requirements of a CTO, and that, above all else, is what I am here to share. As a pragmatist and someone who learns best through doing, I have developed approaches, frameworks, and tools over the years to ensure that when I begin at a new firm, I always hit the ground running.

You will not succeed merely by being a good technologist or a good manager. You must remain intellectually curious, humble, and creative to adapt to the situations and many challenges that you will invariably face. I believe that the CTO role can appear complex and enigmatic, but trust me, it is far simpler than it may seem at first.

I will kick this book off by sharing in greater detail my thoughts on what a CTO actually is. From there, I have divided the rest of the book into four sections: Architecture, Governance, Strategy, and Leadership. I feel these establish the foundational tenets of the role.

The concept of *Architecture* is a somewhat ambiguous, but fully understanding the breadth and depth of this simple term is absolutely foundational to being successful as a CTO. It will drive the development of the various standards and approaches you will need to describe your technology strategies and their alignment with your firm's corporate objectives. It will ensure there is consistency and cohesion across the technology workforce, helping consolidate solutions and maximize reuse. Ultimately, it will ensure that you are able to secure appropriate investments and provide evidence of the benefits. It is really, really important.

The word *Governance* may prompt an involuntary yawn—I get it. However, unless you are a mom-and-pop shop, you will need mechanisms to ensure that you can provide appropriate oversight of the technology workforce and the solutions it delivers. At Citigroup, this meant tens of thousands of technologists, all working independently of one another, all delivering value to their business lines, and all very happy to "innovate" and do things their own way.

Developing appropriate policies, standards, and oversight is necessary to ensure cohesion and mobility across the workforce and will help ensure that everyone is doing *the right things in the right way*. An approach to governance that is heavy-handed will breed resentment and invariably result in the most innovative engineers finding ways to work around your approach. Perhaps even worse, a too simple or lightweight approach will introduce unnecessary bureaucracy and friction without any of the benefits that good governance should deliver. Proper governance should help developers, not hinder them, while ensuring appropriate controls and oversight at the same time.

Next, without the ability to communicate your *Strategy*, you will have limited success as a CTO. You must be able to communicate effectively to all levels of your firm—from C-suite executives to the engineers delivering the solutions—ensuring that everyone understands their responsibilities. Your strategies must be connected and comprehensive to support the realization of your firm's objectives. When defining your strategies, you must consider the level of investment and the time frames needed to implement them. You must also be cognizant of the levels of risk your strategies may introduce and how best to mitigate them. Finally, honestly assess whether your organization is ready to execute them, and if it is not, determine how best to reorganize it while recognizing the operational risks this process may introduce.

Finally, a CTO is not just another technology manager. They are *the* principal technology leader for the firm. As such, it is important to understand, display, and reinforce the traits and behaviors of *Leadership*. You must be able to inspire. You must be able to instill trust. You must be adaptable and innovative in all you do. Even if you have created a perfect approach to architecture, established effective governance, and developed brilliant technology strategies, you will end up on the precipice of failure if you can't capture the hearts and minds of your technology workforce.

Now that I've outlined a broad description of what this book will cover, I should briefly discuss its target audience.

If you're part of a smaller technology organization, your current mission is probably designing, building, and deploying the best possible solution that you can. Your focus may not yet be on the rigorous architecture, governance, and strategy frameworks in this book—or at least not yet. However, if your organization continues to grow, move into new markets, acquire investors, or operate in regulated sectors, then the techniques and frameworks I discuss here will soon be of great importance to you.

If you're already operating within a large-scale enterprise, whether in a regulated sector or not, then this book is definitely for you. In the forthcoming chapters, I'll provide creative solutions to some of the gnarly challenges that you may already be facing. Above all, I hope that these solutions will underpin your future success.

Throughout this book I'll discuss several important strategies I've effectively leveraged in my career, along with examples of where they made—and still make—sense. Above all, my aim is to give you something I wish I would have had at the start of my career: a resource that's comprehensive, helpful, and actionable. With that said, let's get started.

CHAPTER 1

WHAT EXACTLY IS A CTO?

Information technology and business are becoming inextricably interwoven. I don't think anybody can talk meaningfully about one without the talking about the other.

—BILL GATES

Chief technology officers (CTOs) differ from many other key executives and leaders in a company, as not only are they expected to lead and develop the technology strategies that drive commercial success, but they must also ensure that their vision and approach are well understood and supported by the other executives, which, if the business is not a technology firm, can be challenging.

Technology is now ubiquitous across all industries, but the level of comprehension surrounding it has not advanced at the same pace and is still sadly lacking across many senior and board-level executives. Nevertheless, for the role to be successful, it is imperative that the technology vision, strategies, operating model, and risks are all well understood and backed by your firm's senior leadership team to ensure that the necessary commitments are made. This will require the ability to effectively and precisely communicate with all layers of the organization, as well as with external stakeholders. Simply put, communication is one of a CTO's most fundamental responsibilities.

A CTO must be able to abstract and summarize detailed and technical topics appropriately while maintaining the substance and necessary evidence to support the communication. Detailed strategies must exist, appropriate methodologies for sustained success must be in place and credible, and actionable plans and progress metrics must be available. This is the crux of a CTO's responsibilities.

It is worth exploring how the responsibilities of a CTO may differ from those of a chief information officer (CIO), as there is often a good deal of overlap between the two. Both are responsible for delivering technology solutions and managing technology staff. In many technology firms, there is only a CTO who has complete responsibility for all aspects of technology operations. In contrast, more traditional enterprises tend to have a CIO to fulfill these responsibilities.

A useful distinction that I have drawn in my career is that the CIO tends to be responsible for *what* technology products are delivered, while the CTO is responsible for *how* those technology products are delivered. As such, the CTO will *define* an organization's technology policies and standards that must be met, while the CIO will *operate* their procedures to ensure adherence to the standards. Though this is not a hard-and-fast rule, it has been consistent in my experience.

Again, I firmly believe that for the CTO to be successful, they must have *delivery responsibility* to ensure that the policies and standards they introduce are both appropriate and effective. They must consume and operate under the standards they introduce. If not, there is a risk that the standards and procedures are purely "academic" and not practical and fit for purpose. I've seen this happen time and again. When it does, poor adoption of standards, a lack of meaningful governance and oversight, and deficient outcomes inevitably follow.

While it is not difficult to ensure that the CTO has delivery responsibilities, the specific areas to be owned should be considered carefully. I have observed CTOs who have delivery responsibility for implementing their *new strategies* but are not responsible for the operation and maintenance of the *existing solutions* that will be displaced. It is easy to introduce a new solution when you are not obligated to consider migration from the old system and the operational risks and costs that this may introduce.

When there's full responsibility in terms of engineering and operational activities, successful outcomes tend to follow. As an example, an organization could assign their CTO to deliver all of the firm's infrastructure services, new and existing: database platforms, public and private cloud services, and end-user solutions. As these services must abide by the same technology standards as the CIO's products, it ensures the appropriateness of relevant policies, standards, and procedures.

This is why, whichever areas that may end up being the CTO's responsibility, they should have full accountability for running and operating the existing solutions *and* developing new replacement solutions. It ensures an appropriate level of attention on the operational aspects of the new solution and ensures that an appropriate migration path from old to new—mitigating operational risks—is developed.

CORE OBJECTIVES

Before we go into the finer details, there are a number of core, fundamental objectives shared by all CTOs, regardless of the structure of the organization they are operating within.

Define a Coherent Target State

First, it is imperative that a coherent target state for an organization be established and well understood if there is to be a chance of ensuring that strategic investments are being appropriately made. What exactly does this mean? Well, a coherent target state must answer two fundamental questions: "Where do we want to be?" and "Are we doing the right things?" I can hear you now: So what exactly does this mean? Coherent means "logical and consistent." This means that when defining an aspirational target state—for the business and technology platforms that your firm intends to leverage—you must be able to describe it in an easy-to-comprehend and communicable fashion. It must continue to be relevant and accurate over the years as investments are made and systems are deployed. If successful, it will provide a lens for assessing the efficacy of these strategic investments, confirming if they are successfully moving us toward our objectives. On occasion, there may be a need for nonstrategic or tactical investments in other areas, and your target state will also help you understand when these are required.

Establish Effective and Consistent Architectural Governance

Consistent architectural governance is critical to ensure that the investments being made are moving the technology portfolio toward meeting your firm's business objectives while ensuring compliance with the various nonfunctional imperatives that must be met, including security, resilience, and performance issues. A well-designed governance process can ensure that investments are prioritized appropriately, create opportunities for the reuse and consolidation of existing solutions, and ultimately drive cost reductions and improve development velocity. However, it is of paramount importance that the governance activities are relevant and integrated into investment and engineering activities. If not, governance tends to get circumnavigated or outright ignored. Evidence of governance outputs must not only be readily available and easily traced to your end products; they must also be useful and integral to the processes they support.

Improve the Transparency and Quality of Architecture and Design Activities

If the goal of the objective *Define a Coherent Target State* answers the question "Are we doing the right thing?", it is equally important that we answer the question, "Are we doing things the right way?" This ensures that the resultant deliverables meet the resilience, security, and control objectives of your firm and that solutions are sustainable and effectively supported over multiple years and many investment cycles.

Technologists naturally want to focus on the next "big thing," but in reality the technology assets of most firms tend to operate successfully for many years, with the support of evolving teams. Clear and concise design documentation, code annotation, and test plans will ensure the successful maintenance of your assets over successive "generations" of teams supporting them.

Codify Standards and Controls

There are significant benefits to encoding standards and controls into tooling and executing platforms in an automated and preventative manner. This maximizes the control environment while minimizing the friction introduced to the engineering teams. With this model, adherence to standards is implicit. The alternative tends to be manual processes that rely on "trust and verify" models, where quality assurance sampling or internal audits are the mechanisms by which adherence to standards is evidenced. This evidence is incomplete at best and unreliable at worst.

Foster a Culture of Innovation and Engineering Excellence

It is essential that you foster a culture of innovation and general engineering excellence if you expect your technology organization to be able to attract and retain the highest caliber and diversity of staff. A culture of collaboration and evolution must be nurtured. As the Bill Gates quote I used to introduce this chapter suggests, sustainable technology success is of vital importance to any firm's ability to meet its business objectives. In tech, innovation is a constant. Only by ensuring that your technology staff have the support and controls to explore and innovate will new technologies and innovations be adopted and competitive advantages be realized.

KEY CHALLENGES

Beyond the shared objectives that all CTOs have to meet, there will be a number of common challenges that, depending on the organizational structure and history of your firm, an incoming CTO may need to overcome. These challenges are not insurmountable—and there may be many others, depending on your organization's culture, maturity, and business strategy—but being aware of them will enable you to effectively address them.

The CTO Can Be Perceived as Insensitive to Business Objectives

As you focus on ensuring that "things are done the right way," the teams and areas focused on doing "the right things" for the businesses they support may often perceive the CTO office as unappreciative of their challenges and even as impeding their ability to deliver value to their businesses.

Having Impact Without the Necessary Authority

Depending on the organizational structure, the CTO may be one of several technology leaders within a firm, but you must be able to exert appropriate impact and influence throughout the entire organization. It is your responsibility to ensure that policies and standards are appropriately applied and that consistent platforms are adopted. This can be more challenging when you do not have direct authority over those you need to influence.

Standards and Governance Oversight Are Often Perceived as Overly Bureaucratic and Inefficient

This is common in many organizations, especially those that operate in highly regulated industries. Often the standards focus on ease of evidence rather than ease of execution. This approach makes it easy for risk and control officers to show compliance but often makes adherence cumbersome for technology teams, and as a result, they tend to ignore or work around the standards.

Standardization Is Seen as "Change for Change's Sake"

A core objective is to drive efficiency and improve controls, and this can be best achieved by driving consolidation onto consistent platforms and services. Why? This approach concentrates investments and risk oversight activities. However, the benefits to the individual technology team are often not as apparent, so these activities—migration onto shared platforms and services—are perceived to have little value for the teams, even though they present significant holistic benefits to the broader firm.

Consistency Is Seen as an Inhibitor of Innovation

It is natural for talented developers and technical staff to want to adopt new, exciting technologies as soon as they emerge. A consequence of this, if left unchecked, is that many different technologies and solutions can be brought into your firm, creating inconsistency and increasing risk. It is your responsibility to control divergence from standard solutions, but as a result, you may be perceived as an inhibitor of innovation.

PART I
ARCHITECTURE

CHAPTER 2

DEFINING ARCHITECTURE

Any intelligent fool can make things bigger, more complex, and more violent. It takes a touch of genius—and a lot of courage—to move in the opposite direction.

—E. F. SCHUMACHER

I realized very early on that the CTO had to oversee the *Architecture* activities at a firm, so I spent some considerable time researching what exactly architecture meant with regard to technology products.

Although there were, and still are, many definitions of architecture, contradictions and inconsistencies in these descriptions are easy to find. Is Data Architecture the same as Information Architecture? What distinguishes Systems from Solutions Architecture? Does Enterprise Architecture relate to Business Architecture? Is Business Architecture part of Functional Architecture or vice versa? I quickly realized that these subdefinitions matter less than promoting a well-understood definition of architecture at a broad level and then applying it consistently across related activities.

Why is this so important? A comprehensive and unambiguous understanding of what exactly architecture means is foundational to the development of *appropriate* policies, standards, and procedures necessary to provide *effective* oversight of the development of technology products. Imprecision and inconsistency make it difficult to demonstrate appropriate coverage of the required activities. Worse, they can introduce cumbersome or unnecessary (and often unhelpful) policies and procedures, creating inefficiencies in the development process and contributing to organizational reluctance or even resentment toward the governance approach.

As mentioned previously, a cursory investigation will lead to many definitions of architecture. The Gartner IT Glossary[4] has the following definition:

> **Architecture** *is defined as:*
>
> 1. *In reference to computers, software, or networks, the overall design of a computing system and the logical and physical interrelationships between its components. The architecture specifies the hardware, software, access methods, and protocols used throughout the system.*
>
> 2. *A framework and set of guidelines to build new systems. IT architecture is a series of principles, guidelines, or rules used by an enterprise to direct the process of acquiring, building, modifying, and interfacing IT resources throughout the enterprise. These resources can include equipment, software, communications, development methodologies, modeling tools, and organizational structures.*

On the face of it, this provides a comprehensive description. Architecture provides logical and physical interrelationships between components in a system. It specifies that the hardware, software, access methods, and protocols must be defined, and it should provide the framework, principles, and guidelines necessary to build systems. Although this definition appears detailed, it lacks precision when considering exactly what the framework would be. So let's take a look at a couple of the established architecture frameworks that exist instead.

TOGAF[5]

The best-recognized industry standard for *Enterprise Architecture* is TOGAF, or The Open Group Architecture Framework, which was introduced in 1995 and has been refined over a number of years by a global consortium of more than nine hundred organizations. This comprehensive body of knowledge outlines fundamental practices and approaches to all aspects of architecture, including twenty-three specific TOGAF Series Guides[6] that cover specific areas, including business models, business capabilities, business scenarios, and more.

Zachman Enterprise Architecture[7]

In 1987, IT pioneer John Zachman developed an early enterprise architectural method to address the problems facing IT-driven businesses. It differs from TOGAF in that it provides an enterprise ontology: a formal and structured classification system for defining an enterprise. Zachman's schema is oriented toward organizing architectural artifacts—it's not a methodology, nor does it define specific approaches for collecting, managing, or using the data it collects.

I do not proclaim to be an expert in either of these frameworks; these are but two of the most well known. There are many others developed by consortia, governments, and proprietary to specific firms, including the *Generalised Enterprise Reference Architecture and Methodology*, the *US Department of Defense Architecture Framework*, and the *Federal Enterprise Architecture Framework*, to name a few.

I strongly encourage you to investigate some of these frameworks and approaches, as there will undoubtedly be insights and utility in doing so. It may introduce concepts or artifacts that are useful to you. However, I quickly recognized that there were inconsistencies across these frameworks—Enterprise Architecture was often used synonymously with Business Architecture, ignoring other fundamental domains that must be addressed. Some frameworks provided only definitional taxonomies and ontologies.

Moreover, there are well-recognized weaknesses in any formal Enterprise Architecture frameworks, as independent researcher Svyatoslav Kotusev detailed in his 2016 article, "Enterprise Architecture Frameworks: The Fad of the Century."[8] He identified that the documentation provided was often "too conceptual, inflexible, incomprehensible and obsolete to be useful"; that "huge efforts and resources are needed to develop and maintain EA documentation"; and especially that "EA-related activities happen in 'ivory towers', EA documentation is ignored."

I experienced this early on after inheriting a large Enterprise Architecture team as the CTO of a major European bank. After thoroughly investigating this all for myself, it did not take long to realize that I needed a simple and comprehensive definition of architecture. This would enable me to establish appropriate boundaries between development activities and ensure unambiguous and relevant utility, communication, and governance. It was important that whatever was introduced integrated with—and was useful to—the designers and developers who were delivering solutions. It could not be an exercise in prescribed documentation that did not connect to the actual developer practices in place. If it were to become orthogonal and incremental to those processes, then the likelihood of adoption, accuracy, and utility would be significantly diminished.

ARCHITECTURE DISCIPLINES AND LEVELS

Underpinning my definition of architecture are two fairly basic concepts that must be understood: first, there are a number of distinct *disciplines of architecture*, each requiring different skills and expertise; second, there are different *levels of architecture* that are necessary to communicate effectively with different roles within the organization.

Each of the disciplines will occur at different levels, albeit with varying degrees of importance. There should be a clear lineage between artifacts—business proposals, requirements, technical specifications, and more—at every level. When higher levels clearly delegate to lower levels, your team will be able to logically follow strategic intentions down through their implementation deliverables.

Architecture Disciplines

For simplicity's sake, I decided to define five interrelated *disciplines* of architecture, each of which represents a specific architectural area of expertise and requires a different set of skills. Significantly, there are likely to be very different policies, standards, and oversight required for each. They are as follows:

> **Business:** This defines the processes and functions necessary to *describe* the operations and activities of your firm,

which are required to realize the strategic business objectives. As an example, in any client-oriented industry, there will likely be a business process to onboard a new client or settle a complaint.

Information: This defines the data concepts and models, both logical and physical, to describe the data assets needed to support the business processes. To extend our prior example, if there is a business process to onboard a new client, it will likely require data to describe the client, their location, and perhaps the products they are using.

Application: This defines how an application is structured, technically and operationally to (1) meet the functional objectives defined by the Business and Information architecture, and (2) meet nonfunctional considerations such as resilience, performance, and operational needs. For example, one may need specific applications that support adding a client, amending an address, or registering a complaint.

Technology: This defines the executing environment in which all applications run, including all infrastructural services, such as compute, storage, and networking, that host the applications. As an example, this includes defining the use of public cloud services such as Amazon Web Services or Azure.

Security: This defines how the necessary security controls are integrated into the data, applications, and hosting environment to ensure that all aspects of confidentiality, integrity, and security are met. If we are building in the public cloud, this will include ensuring that the data, applications, and hosting environment are secure and protected against nefarious actors.

These disciplines have cleanly delineated responsibilities, and each will depend on a variety of subject matter experts. For example, the expert defining the Logical Data Models required for Information Architecture is unlikely to be the same as the expert defining your firm's security requirements and capabilities as part of Security Architecture. Each of these disciplines requires the development of discipline-specific policies, standards, and procedures and the requisite governance oversight. At the same time, it's imperative that each discipline is well understood and sensibly related to the others.

Architecture Levels

Each discipline may need to provide specific types of artifacts at different *levels* of the organization, with different target audiences and objectives at each level. We can simplify this by broadly defining the following three *levels* of architecture:

Enterprise: The highest level of architecture, concerned with defining the approach toward successfully executing the business strategy and realizing key objectives. At this level, where many disparate business processes and capabilities must be defined, there is a need for consistency and fidelity across the enterprise. This helps identify areas of commonality that offer opportunities for consolidation and reuse and ensures consistency in describing key risks and issues that may need to be addressed. At this level the audience for the outputs tends to be senior stakeholders, both internal and external to the firm, who make strategic investment decisions, track the progress of prior investments, and ensure the resolution of specific concerns.

Solutions: The next level of architecture, which is concerned with describing the specific solutions needed to address identified business and functional deliverables. A variety of artifacts are needed, at a level of fidelity that can support the design and planning of the solution. At this level the audience tends to be the specific business leaders who own the solution, as well as the implementation team.

Software: The lowest level of architecture, which describes the detailed specifications necessary to implement the solution. It must have sufficient detail to ensure that the implementation meets the functional and nonfunctional requirements of the solution. At this level the audience tends to be the technical staff responsible for the execution and operation of the application.

The following figure provides a representation of how these disciplines and levels relate. Although all disciplines of architecture are relevant to all the levels, there is a greater reliance on some at each level, which is represented in the diagram by the degrees of shading.

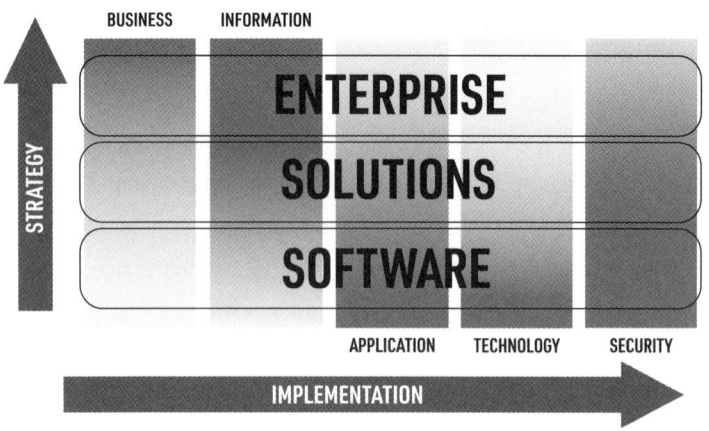

THE DISCIPLINES AND LEVELS OF ARCHITECTURE

You will notice that both Business and Information Architecture are essential to the development of the Enterprise Architecture artifacts that underpin your firm's *strategy*. This requires an understanding of your business capabilities, processes, and functions, along with the related data concepts. Without these details, any strategic intent would be vaporous. There is *less* need—but not zero need—for details on the Technology Architecture at this level, as many technologies could be adopted to implement a given strategy. Conversely, at the Software Level, there is a huge dependency on the Application, Technology, and Security Architecture disciplines but less need for Information Architecture and little need for the Business Architecture discipline as the activities move toward *implementation*.

What is of paramount importance is recognizing that all the implementation specifics only exist to materialize the strategic objectives outlined as part of Enterprise Architecture—predominantly leveraging the Business and Information Architecture disciplines—while the solutions are implemented as part of Software Architecture—predominantly leveraging the Application, Technology, and Security Architecture disciplines, as the diagram that follows shows. If you find that you are implementing items that cannot be traced back to the strategic objectives, then something is amiss.

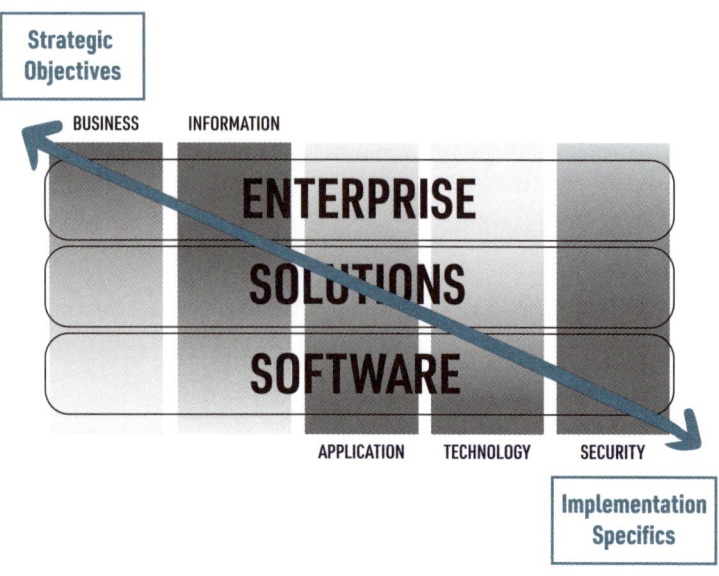

STRATEGIC OBJECTIVES REALIZED BY IMPLEMENTATION SPECIFICS

Whenever I have introduced this definition, confusion has most often arisen in understanding the different *levels* of architecture, as the disciplines are easier to comprehend because they are somewhat self-describing. Some assume that the levels here relate to the *level of detail required*, with less detail at the Enterprise Level and much more at the Software Level. This is not true: detail and fidelity are required at *all* levels.

An analogy that I have returned to often will help clarify. Imagine that you are in the International Space Station (ISS), observing the planet Earth below you. You can see the whole of the planet as you orbit it, able to recognize the continents, oceans, and the shapes of individual countries. Beyond this, you have various sensors and cameras at your disposal, each of which sharpens your observations of what is happening below.

One day you observe two areas of the planet where huge plumes of smoke are being released into the atmosphere. The exact cause is unclear, but your sensors indicate extreme temperatures, so some type of fire is the likely cause. You call down to alert mission control, and they dispatch two reconnaissance aircraft to go and investigate. At the first location, their plane identifies a huge forest fire. At the second location, they encounter a volcanic eruption. Both events initially appear to be identical, but upon closer inspection, they have very different root causes.

At the first event, a ground crew of firefighters is quickly dispatched to help fight the fire, and on the ground, the firefighters quickly devise a detailed plan on how to contain the fire and bring it under control, building firebreaks and coordinating firefighting plans. At the site of the volcanic eruption, a different solution is required. Local law enforcement coordinates to ensure everyone in the vicinity is evacuated and moved to safety. Both of the on-the-ground activities are successful, albeit very different in their approaches to what, at first impression, seemed to be identical events.

In this example the observers in the ISS are analogous to Enterprise Architects. They have a consistent and normalized view that enables them to identify "hot spots" where further investigation or intervention may be necessary. At the same time, they lack the finer details necessary to determine exactly what the solution should be on the ground.

Mission control is analogous to key stakeholders—they decide *where* to act. The crew of the reconnaissance aircraft are analogous to Solutions Architects. They assess the specific solutions that will be required, understanding the specifics of the challenges that need to be addressed.

Finally, the firefighters and local law enforcement on the ground are analogous to the Software Architects. They determine the specific implementation of the solution needed, making strategic and tactical decisions accordingly as they deliver the right solution to address the on-the-ground challenges.

At this point I have no doubt that established practitioners of one or more of the previously mentioned Enterprise Architecture frameworks will identify and declare similarities to their chosen framework. This is unsurprising, as I have been influenced by them all. However, I have found that, in practice, the preceding is simple enough to explain to all personas within an organization—from detailed-oriented technology developers to more senior stakeholders who do not come from a technology background—while also providing sufficient structure to drive robust governance and development practices. It has served me well.

In the forthcoming chapters, I will explore the different disciplines of architecture and provide insights on frameworks that may be applicable at each level. To be clear, there is not necessarily a framework at the intersection of every discipline and level. Furthermore, my intention is *not* to prescribe a set of documentation that you must produce, as many other Enterprise Architecture approaches tend to do. Rather, by delineating discrete focus areas and a purpose for the respective *disciplines* of architecture—and by sharing what's worked for me—you'll be able to meld the existing mechanisms you may have in place while introducing new processes where it makes sense. You will, at the very least, understand my rationale for their introduction.

CHAPTER 3
BUSINESS ARCHITECTURE

*If you don't know where you are going,
every road will get you nowhere.*
—HENRY KISSINGER

Business Architecture is one of the better-described domains of architecture. It is most closely aligned with the practice of Enterprise Architecture, as it focuses on defining the needs and strategic objectives of the specific business that is being supported. The Business Architecture Center of Excellence[9] has the following succinct description:

> **Business Architecture** *is explicitly representing an organization's desired state and as-is state, through a set of independent, non-redundant artifacts, defining how these artifacts relate with each other and developing a set of prioritized, aligned capabilities needed to meet the organization's goals, communicating this understanding to stakeholders, and advancing the organization from its as-is state to its desired state.*

This description brings forward a number of core principles that are worth reviewing. First, Business Architecture describes the need for a *desired state* for the entire organization and an understanding of the organization's current *as-is state*. As simple as this sounds, defining these states can be incredibly challenging in practice. Even a relatively small organization will have a myriad of business capabilities and processes at different levels of maturity.

Once you've managed this first step, your next task is to develop *a set of prioritized, aligned capabilities needed to meet your organization's goals*. No organization has truly unlimited resources, and because of this, they must establish a consistent approach in describing their current and required capabilities. Every business needs to do this before making the necessary judgments in terms of where investments should be made.

Next, it's important to track your investments' efficacy in advancing the organization from its as-is state to its desired state. Are the strategic objectives being realized within acceptable variances of the originally planned projected investments?

With all this in mind, it's worth considering the responsibilities of Business Architecture at the different levels of architecture.

BUSINESS ARCHITECTURE AT THE ENTERPRISE LEVEL

You will need a carefully calibrated framework to describe the existing and required business capabilities for an enterprise, assess where the biggest "bang for your bucks" may be, and then effectively track the progression of the investment to the realization of your objectives.

Over many years I have developed an approach to systematically define the necessary artifacts for Business Architecture at the

Enterprise Level. It is fairly simple to describe, but implementation requires rigor and firm-wide commitment.

1. At the foundation there is a need to create consistent and nonvolatile **taxonomies** to describe the core concepts of your organization. This will primarily include business processes, functions, and data concepts, but there may be others that you deem necessary for your firm, such as products, controls, and more.

2. These taxonomies can then be leveraged to define your organization's **target state**—that is, your business capabilities and the deliverables that are required for success. It entails "blue sky" thinking on what you want your organization to achieve, *unconstrained* by its current capabilities. This is extremely hard to do, but once you have your target state in place, it should not change markedly unless it is forced to as a result of a drastic shift in your business objectives or strategy.

3. At the Enterprise Architecture level, I *do not* define the **as-is state** of the organization. Why? In my opinion it simply tends to be futile. I have seen many architects happily get lost in this activity. Organizations are always in a state of flux and change as investments are made and capabilities are developed. It is their very nature. If you were to create a detailed current state model, then maintaining it would require huge, continual effort. It is one of the contributing factors to the previously cited observation by Kotusev that "huge efforts and resources are needed to develop and maintain EA documentation."

4. Instead, take the time to define the **key indicators and measures** that allow you to assess how far you currently are from the desired target state. In this way you can identify relevant hot spots or areas where you wish to progress to the next level of maturity, whether that entails developing new capabilities or addressing the shortcomings of an existing one.

5. Once you are able to decide where your next investments should be made, you can define the **as-is state** of that business capability at the *level of Solutions Architecture*. Here, as we are describing a very specific area of the organization, as opposed to the whole enterprise, an appropriate level of detail can be captured, and you can make informed decisions on how best to advance toward your desired end state.

The preceding are the logical steps that should be progressed by an organization's Enterprise Architects. It is important to maintain strict change control on the resultant artifacts. If you don't, it is hard to point to the specific drivers of progress. A stable baseline is required to prove that advancements are a direct result of investments, not the result of changes made to these artifacts.

Taxonomies

Foundational to Business Architecture is the creation of an appropriate language to describe the business capabilities. It can be as extensive as you deem necessary, but in my experience, the following are the three core taxonomies that must be created and maintained:

Business Processes: These are the unique and distinct business activities that produce a discernible output, either to clients or as an input to another process.

Business Functions: These are the specific activities that occur within a business process. The key thing to remember here is that the same function may support several business processes.

Derived from the Information Architecture discipline, there will also be the following:

Data Concepts: These are the discrete inputs and outputs of a business function and, ultimately, a business process. They describe the core data assets required.

As with most taxonomies, there is probably a need for hierarchical classifications to organize and disambiguate relevant terms. Don't go overboard and introduce more complexity here than you need. I've found that three levels are sufficiently rich to provide appropriate context for the leaf node, or the lowest level of the hierarchy.

As a simple contrived example, let's consider a business process for an *Employee Complaint*. This would likely be one of several processes related to employees, such as *Onboard New Employee* or *Exit Existing Employee*. These could all be part of the *Employee-Related* process group, which would fall under the category of *Human Resources*. The resultant hierarchy for the actual employee complaint process would be as follows:

Human Resources > Employee Related > Employee Complaint

There will also be an ontology or relationships that exist between the core taxonomies. Expanding on the example of the employee complaint process, it may consist of a number of functions to logically implement it, such as *Add New Complaint* or *Find Existing Complaint*. Similarly, for these functions to be useful, they need to use or produce some data. The Add New Complaint function would most likely logically emit a new *Complaint* data concept, whereas the Find Existing Complaint may logically require the *Employee* data concept as an input.

This figure illustrates the relationships between core taxonomies:

It is important to recognize that these relationships are not unique. For example, a *Client Complaint* process would also leverage the Add New Complaint and Find Existing Complaint functions, albeit the data concepts to find a Complaint would likely be *Client* and not *Employee*.

This is powerful to recognize because the shared functions could be engineered in a way that supports both business processes—in this case by creating an abstract *Person* data concept that would include either a Client or an Employee. In that way there would be a consolidated solution, minimizing the investment needed to support both business processes and helping to drive consistency in solutions.

I draw the distinction from which discipline these taxonomies align with to ensure that, as further artifacts are developed within

30 THE CREATIVE CTO

a specific architectural discipline, appropriate *lineage* can be maintained to the artifacts created at the lower levels. As an example, the data concepts will be further elaborated to create Logical and Physical Data Models, as we will see later in the "Information Architecture" chapter.

One area that is often considered but should *not* be included here is *organizational structure*. Business processes and functions should be agnostic to the organization that currently executes them. Simply put, they should be generalized and not dependent on the current organization. This ensures that any existing organizational constraints do not impede the development of your taxonomies, the "We don't do that today!" paradigm.

I have found that these core concepts provide appropriate foundations to begin to model the target state. These can then be the basis for subsequent enrichments should other taxonomies make sense. Please remember, while your business will constantly be in flux, your taxonomy should remain relatively fixed.

Target State

Defining the target state for an organization at the Enterprise Architecture level should strike a delicate balance. On one hand, it should represent the enterprise at a sufficiently high level of abstraction so that it can be normalized and considered as one. On the other hand, it should be detailed enough to allow an assessment of the maturity—that is, how close the current organization is to its desired target state.

Over the years I have assessed a number of different approaches to best describe the target state. These have ranged from pseudo-detailed wiring diagrams that relate to databases and applications to highly abstract "enterprise-on-a-page" representations that show only the highest level of data movement. The former, while useful at the Solutions or Software Level of architecture, rarely aids in making concise explanations to sponsors and stakeholders at the Enterprise Level. The latter are perfect for providing an abridged Enterprise Architecture view of how an organization is meeting the needs of its sponsors but become untenable when trying to connect to the lower levels of architecture.

It took me some time to find an acceptable middle ground. In the end my needs were met with an adapted version of a diagrammatic approach developed in the 1950s: the *functional block diagram*. This provided sufficient abstraction *and* the ability to connect and show lineage to the details required at the lower levels.

Leveraging a Functional Block Diagram

A functional block diagram is a graphical representation that describes a number of functions, which are represented as blocks, and the interrelationships between them. The following are five steps that allow us to leverage it as a mechanism to describe a target state:

1. Create a single diagram that represents the target state of a specific *business process*.

2. Within this business process, create a number of blocks, each of which represents a specific *function* within the process.

3. Illustrate key *data concepts* for each function, identifying them as either inputs or outputs. These ultimately describe the interrelationships between the functions in the process.

4. Identify data concepts that cannot be traced to other functions within the business process. These concepts are either (1) from outside this business process and thus an

input to the process as a whole, or (2) explicitly captured within the function as data entries.

5. Conclude the business process by specifying that it emits one or more data concepts for consumption by other business processes or is a terminus that returns outputs to a consumer.

A simple representation of this can be seen below:

<BUSINESS PROCESS NAME>

<Data Concept> → <FUNCTION> → <Data Concept> → <FUNCTION> → <Data Concept>

<Data Concept> → <FUNCTION> → <Data Concept>

BUSINESS PROCESS TEMPLATE LEVERAGING FUNCTIONS AND DATA CONCEPTS

This illustration shows an unnamed business process that has two distinct data concepts as inputs, each input for two functions that form part of the broader process. These functions both emit distinct data concepts, which act as inputs to a third function. The resultant data concept that function emits is also the output of the whole business process.

To demonstrate how this works in practice, let's consider an extremely basic and contrived example of a business process called *Credit Card Issuing*. This process reviews an applicant's request for a new product and uses a simple set of functions—*Identity Check*,

Check Credit Score, Fraud Detections, and *Applicant Approval*—to complete the evaluation. It utilizes data concepts, such as *Applicant, Product, Credit Bureau,* and *Score.* It is followed by the *Credit Card Production* process.

<CREDIT CARD ISSUING>

EXAMPLE OF BUSINESS PROCESS - CREDIT CARD ISSUING

This representation is extremely simple but demonstrates how a logical description of the business process can be created. It makes no assumptions on the technologies used, the manual activities that may exist in the current process, or the details with regard to the data sources. It merely describes an idealized representation of the logical steps required, as well as the broad data concepts that would be required.

It is important to reiterate that these business process diagrams model a desired end state or target state and not necessarily the functions or flows that may be in place *now*. By focusing on modeling the target states, in addition to the creation of the target state itself, other core outcomes can be achieved.

As previously mentioned the appropriateness and completeness of the taxonomies can be validated: Are there superfluous functions or data concepts not leveraged in a target state diagram that should be dropped from the taxonomy? Have you identified a need for additional business processes not previously identified? This process helps demonstrate the efficacy and appropriateness of both your defined taxonomies and the target state diagrams.

In the end, remember that the core outcome of developing a target state diagram is to provide a device to *assess the maturity of your current solutions*.

Assessing Maturity of the Current State—Mapping Assets

Enterprise Architecture assessments should help you understand where opportunities exist for improvements to be made. That may entail simplifying existing systems or data stores, reducing major incidents, or eliminating dependencies on manual activities to support business processes. These assessments must be made with certainty that they accurately reflect the enterprise at a given point in time, allowing you to track the momentum of change as you move from your current state to your desired state. The sad reality is that, more often than not, the expected outcomes from strategic initiatives may not always be realized. A credible approach must recognize this and *accurately* report progress, for better or worse.

Once you've (a) created an accurate set of foundational taxonomies, (b) validated them through appropriate target state diagrams, and (c) ensured they reflect how the business capabilities of an organization *should* operate, the next step is to map your *existing* organizational assets to these taxonomies.

Your first task is to map the existing application assets of the organization to the various functions that you have identified. You will very quickly find that there is a mismatch between the applications you *currently* have and the functions required in the target state. Each existing application tends to support more than one of the target functions.

This is unsurprising. Unless your application architecture is based on a microservices[10] approach, the applications are developed over time to support evolving functional needs. They may not all be *monoliths*,[11] but there has been a tendency to consolidate functionality into single application assets, as expanding an existing asset's capabilities sadly is often considered simpler than introducing a new service or application.

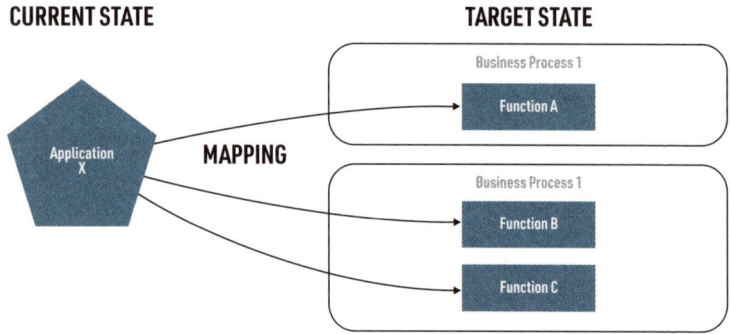

MAPPING EXISTING APPLICATIONS TO TARGET STATE FUNCTIONS

Often a single application is critical to the implementation of multiple functions and, by association, is equally critical to multiple business processes that leverage those functions. Identifying this *concentration risk* is a core Enterprise Architecture assessment.

It is desirable to reduce concentration risk for a number of reasons. First, concentration risk makes the impact of failure much broader than it should be. This is often referred to as the blast radius—the larger the blast radius, the greater the breadth of impact when an application fails. Reducing the blast radius is therefore desirable. Second, when an application supports multiple functions, complexity increases. Different objectives may necessitate changes to different functions implemented by the same application. This may result in complex code and will definitely create a complex development and change management process, as different release schedules and drivers compete with one another.

Beyond identifying application issues, you must map the existing physical *data sources* that these applications consume or emit to the various *data concepts* you have identified. These may be physical data inputs, databases, file transfers, on-the-wire messages, or other mechanisms by which the application receives or produces data. Since you've already mapped applications to functions, the data concepts that the application should map to are those that the target state describes as necessary to support mapped functions. The existing data sources that an application uses subsequently can be mapped to those data concepts. It is common for a specific data source to map to more than one data concept. We should also identify which data sources support multiple applications for the same data concept and, conversely, which data concepts have multiple data sources mapped to them. This is another core Enterprise Architecture Assessment, as it allows us to identify data fragmentation and potential data duplication.

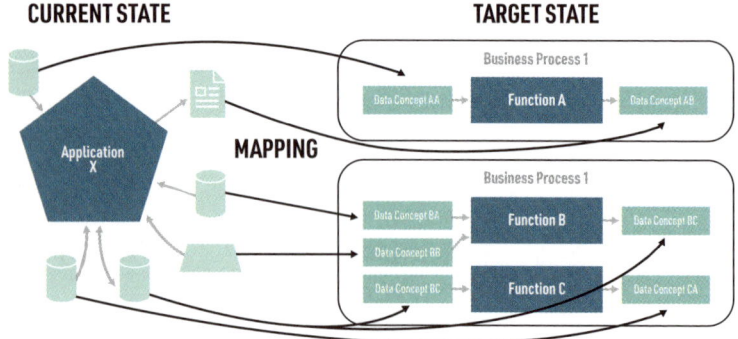

MAPPING EXISTING DATA SOURCES TO TARGET STATE DATA CONCEPTS

You should be able to glean other interesting information from this mapping exercise. The illustration above shows a direct mapping with all the existing application data sources cleanly mapped to the target state data concepts. However, there may be instances where the application currently consumes or produces a data source unmapped to target state data concepts. This could suggest several things: perhaps there is another function that this application supports that has not yet been mapped, or perhaps there is a flaw in the target state model in which an additional data source should be associated with a function. It could also be a superfluous or duplicative data source, a legacy of many iterations of application changes. We cannot conclude from the mapping exercise alone, but we have managed to uncover an area for further investigation and resolution.

Once you have mapped and validated all existing assets to appropriate functions and data concepts, you can make other interesting Enterprise Architecture assessments. Are there target state functions without existing applications that support them, revealing a manual process that may be eliminated? Are there many existing applications that support the same function, suggesting redundancy and duplication, and ultimately presenting an opportunity to consolidate? Where are existing data sources unmapped to data concepts, suggesting legacy or redundant data sources? Are there data concepts without data sources, suggesting dependencies on manual data entry?

Mapped assets—both the databases and applications—also support data enrichment that can drive the assessment process. You can readily assess failures and incidents, operational costs, and third-party dependencies by associating them with the assets in use. Then use this information to identify where to make strategic investments or where there are areas of high risk. You can also map these to the affected business processes that are dependent on the functions that map to the application in question. As you can see, you can derive a substantial amount of Business Architecture intelligence from this simple exercise.

Another important point to note: mapping activity *must* become part of the asset change management process. When you make enhancements that affect an application's mapping to functions or data concepts, you will need to accurately reflect these changes. This approach allows you to maintain a consistent representation of the current state, as well as assess how effectively strategic investments and programs are *advancing the organization toward its desired state*.

Tracking Progress

Tracking progress is critical for establishing a credible Business Architecture approach. Taxonomies can provide a mechanism to group and organize key metrics and can demonstrate momentum of change and progress. Using taxonomies in conjunction with mapped assets will introduce manageable metrics that suggest simplification and consolidation. These are key objectives for any enterprise and tend to result in lower costs, improved operational efficiency, and greater resiliency. Let's explore some relevant metrics.

Functional Precision Ratios: Ideally, each function required in your target state would be supported by exactly one technology application. Why? Because this means that functional enhancements and nonfunctional improvements can be concentrated on a single asset. This eliminates duplicative spending, reduces change activity, and concentrates the operational overhead into a single operational asset.

This can be represented by a simple ratio as follows:

Enterprise Functional Precision = Number of Instances of Mapped Applications / Total Number of Functions

This provides an aggregated number for the whole enterprise, in which the same application may be mapped to many functions. At the same time, some functions may not have any applications mapped to them. For example, let's assume you require 100 functions, with 600 instances of applications being mapped to those functions. Your ratio in this case would be 600/100, or 6.0. At a macro level, this suggests that there is significant opportunity for simplification, as the ratio is not 1.0. At this point, however, where to actually focus is somewhat still unclear.

Here, it is important to disaggregate this into a more meaningful *grain size*, even if you maintain this top-level metric as an indicator of firm-wide "health." The groupings of functions that relate to a specific business process provide a very meaningful lens to assess things.

A metric to do this could be defined as follows:

Business Process Functional Precision = Number of Instances of Mapped Applications to the Functions in the Business Process / Number of Functions in the Business Process

This provides a mechanism for comparison *across* business processes. For example, if business process A has 15 functions defined in its target state and 30 instances of mapped applications, then its ratio would be 30/15, or 2.0. Assuming this process is part of the same example as previously stated for the enterprise, this is considerably better than the Enterprise Functional Precision of 6.0. Likewise, if business process B were to have 4 functions defined in its target state and 40 mapped applications, its ratio would be 40/4, or 10.0. This is worse than the other business process and above the enterprise average, indicating that this area should be prioritized.

To be clear, as we have previously defined, this is an Enterprise Architecture assessment. It has identified relative areas of interest or concern, but until we dig deeper, we do not know for certain that business process B is indeed more complicated than it needs to be. There may be business or regulatory reasons for multiple applications to support the same function, such as the need for country-specific implementations. Further analysis is needed, but now we at least have a good idea of where to look.

Monolith Ratio: This ratio examines the total number of applications supported by an enterprise and compares them with the number of times they are mapped to a discrete function. In this way we can determine whether we are dependent on monoliths, a term that refers to a single application supporting many disparate functions. Monoliths tend to be associated with greater complexity and increased fragility during change.

The metric for this could be defined as follows:

Enterprise Monolith Ratio = Number of Unique Mapped Applications / Total Number of Applications Available

In the prior metric, we were interested in the number of application mappings, regardless if it was the same application mapped to the same function in different business processes. In this instance we want to eliminate those duplications and look for unique mappings from the application to the function, regardless of which business process it occurs in. Similar to the prior metric, this provides an aggregated number for the whole enterprise. So building on our prior example, if we assume that there are 500 instances of applications uniquely mapped to the target state functions and a total of 125 applications available, the ratio would be 500/125, or 4.0. This suggests that on average, every available application supports 4.0 functions.

Again, it may be useful to disaggregate this to a grain size that provides a comparative metric. In this case simply looking at the specific application and the number of unique functions it has been mapped to would provide this:

Total Number of Discrete Functions a Specific Application Is Mapped To

To expand this example, if we find that a specific application is supporting 20 discrete functions through its mapped instances, this would be significantly higher than the enterprise average of 4.0, which would suggest an opportunity for simplification and the decomposition of that monolith application into discrete applications.

Incidents by Process and Function: This is a simple metric that tracks the total number of incidents related to a specific function or associated business process over a predetermined time period (such as monthly). By tracking this number and how it changes over time, you can identify and remediate areas of weakness, whether they are caused by human or technology error.

Data Concept Fragmentation Ratio: In general, the fewer physical sources you have for a specific data concept, the better. And for certain types of data, such as *Reference* or *Master Data* sources, having only one physical source is an extremely desirable end state. Why? Because it ensures consistency in the data structures, including the data life cycle events—that is, the activities that act upon the data, including those that create or change it. Why is this important? Because less variation increases the likelihood of accurate data, which critically underpins all business processes. Any duplication or redundancy will necessitate reconciliation processes to ensure accurate reporting and revenue activities. This increases cost, complexity, and the risks of inaccurate or delayed results.

A simple ratio can define this:

Data Concept Fragmentation = Number of Instances of Mapped Data Concepts / Total Number of Data Concepts

This provides an aggregated number for the whole enterprise, whereby the same data source may be mapped to many data concepts. A data source without any data concepts mapped to it represents a significant anomaly. The same applies to a data concept that does not map to any data sources. Both situations merit prioritized investigation.

Again, it may be useful to disaggregate this to a grain size to provide a comparative metric. In this case, simply looking at specific data concepts and the number of unique data sources to which they have been mapped would provide this:

> Total Number of Discrete Data Sources a
> Specific Data Concept Is Mapped To

This will allow prioritization of which data concepts are the most fragmented across existing data sources and, similarly, identify those data concepts that do not have any mapped data sources, which suggests incomplete mapping or manual data entry.

BUSINESS ARCHITECTURE AT OTHER LEVELS

While the Business discipline is significant at the Enterprise Level, it does not typically extend to additional discipline-specific artifacts at the Solutions and Software Levels. However, as other assets are being developed—the applications, services, and platforms—they must still demonstrate their relevance to your firm's objectives as evidenced by the Business Architecture. How do we achieve this? It is straightforward: once we've developed a rich taxonomy to describe business processes, functions, and data sources, we can ensure appropriate lineage by labeling other assets and artifacts with items from our taxonomy.

For example, as part of the Application discipline, we may develop a specific solution to support a business process. The artifacts, which we will discuss later in the Application Architecture section, should be labeled with this business process. As simple as this sounds, it is incredibly useful. The development costs can be identified and aggregated against the process, and this provides useful insight into determining the total cost of ownership for that process. Likewise, if subsequent detailed specifications are then developed at the Software Level, these can also be labeled with the relevant business process and, better still, the relevant functions from the business process. When we finally create the assets themselves, these, too, can be labeled.

Applying the Business Architecture taxonomies to all other artifacts and assets developed during the other disciplines and levels of architecture ensures lineage and traceability. This is fundamental in demonstrating a coherent target state and helps explain why we are doing what we are doing by tracing back to the developed Business Architecture Target State.

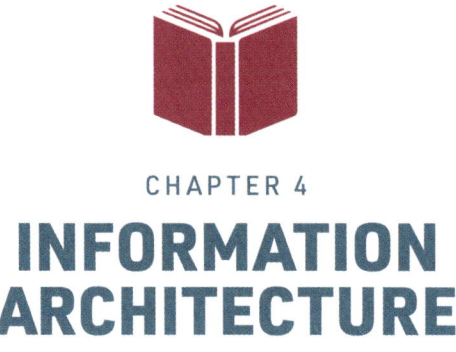

CHAPTER 4

INFORMATION ARCHITECTURE

*You can have data without information,
but you cannot have information without data.*
—DANIEL KEYS MORAN

There has been much debate in the industry regarding Information versus Data Architecture. Are they the same or different? Peter Drucker, a pioneer in modern management theory, once described information as "data endowed with relevance and purpose." The *Harvard Business Review*[12] builds on this to provide the following definitions:

> **Data Architecture** *describes how data is collected, stored, transformed, distributed, and consumed. It includes the rules governing structured formats, such as databases and file systems, and the systems for connecting data with the business processes that consume it.*
>
> **Information Architecture** *governs the processes and rules that convert data into useful information. For example, data architecture might feed raw daily advertising and sales data*

> into information architecture systems, such as marketing dashboards, where it is integrated and analyzed to reveal relationships between ad spend and sales by channel and region.

Unfortunately, this distinction is, at best, adequate, implying that Data Architecture focuses on *raw* data, such as how it is structured, how it is stored, and the physical systems that perform these tasks. By contrast, Information Architecture focuses on governing the processes and rules for consuming and deriving value and insights from the data, shaping it to drive business decisions and outcomes.

In reality, this representation is unsatisfactory. Why? Operational data stores that collect data have intrinsic value to an organization, and they require enrichment and integration with other data sets to effectively drive business processes. Achieving operational efficiency at all stages of the data life cycle necessitates this. For example, data may be captured early in the data life cycle purely to satisfy and streamline business processes later on.

As I outlined in my introduction to architecture, the most important thing is to land on a definition that is *simple and unambiguous*. Creating a delineation between Data and Information Architecture is unnecessary when we apply our earlier definition of architecture, which includes different artifacts and audiences for different levels.

The *Harvard Business Review*'s definition of Information Architecture does align with the Business and Information disciplines at the Enterprise Architecture Level. Here, we need to define data concepts and understand their relationship to business processes and functions. At this level we are unconcerned with the specifics of the data, including where it is stored and exactly how it is defined. What is more important is to understand the data *in the context of its business use*.

Similarly, the definition of Data Architecture aligns with the Information discipline at the Solution Architecture Level. Here, specifics about the logical and physical structure of the data become far more important, as do the data flows between systems. This also aligns with the Application discipline at the Software Architecture Level, when we need to define specifics on systems and data stores.

For simplicity, I have settled on the term "Information Architecture" to cover both concepts. As Daniel Keys Moran makes clear in his quote at the beginning of this chapter, you can have data without information but not vice versa, so Information Architecture feels like the superset of the two. Simplistic? I do hope so.

DATA GOVERNANCE VERSUS DATA MANAGEMENT

Before diving into the specifics of Information Architecture, we must understand and disambiguate *Data Management* and *Data Governance*, as the two are often conflated. Fortunately, these two terms have significantly more consensus on their meaning and distinction. The DAMA International *DAMA-DMBOK* guide[13] is probably the most well-known. This "not-for-profit, vendor-independent, global association of technical and business professionals" is dedicated to advancing the key concepts and practices necessary for information and data management. It provides the following definitions:

> **Data Governance** *exercises authority, control, and shared decision-making about data management.*
>
> **Data Management** *develops, executes, and supervises plans, policies, and programs regarding the maintenance of data assets and supporting their lifecycle.*

Simply put, Data Governance concerns itself with defining governance processes, roles, and responsibilities, all of which dictate how we should define and manage data throughout its life cycle, from creation to archival and deletion. Data Management concerns itself with executing and operating the systems and processes necessary to adhere to governance requirements. These are both important concepts, and they should be evident in your organization.

Business data is a core, foundational asset. With this in mind, Data Governance should fall under the remit of your firm's chief data officer (CDO). The CDO operates on behalf of the various business owners responsible for their data, ensuring that it is appropriately defined to meet the business objectives of your firm and support the various business processes. Data Management, given its reliance on the development of applications, pipelines, stores, and databases, should fall under the remit of the technology head, be it the CIO or CTO. This distinction is subtle but important. A business should own its data assets just as it would any other physical or financial asset. Yet in my experience, firms are often reluctant to do so, preferring to "leave it to technology," an approach that rarely, if ever, succeeds. Understanding this distinction is absolutely crucial for your future success.

EVOLUTION OF INFORMATION AT DIFFERENT LEVELS

Unlike Business Architecture, which is predominantly required at the Enterprise Level, Information Architecture is important at *all* levels. As you descend through the levels, you'll need to elaborate on details, but unambiguous traceability must be maintained.

The diagram below shows a simple representation of core concepts that you should understand. The data concept, introduced as part of Business Architecture, is elaborated as a single, authoritative Logical

Data Model in Solutions Architecture, then further expanded into one or more Physical Data Models required in Software Architecture.

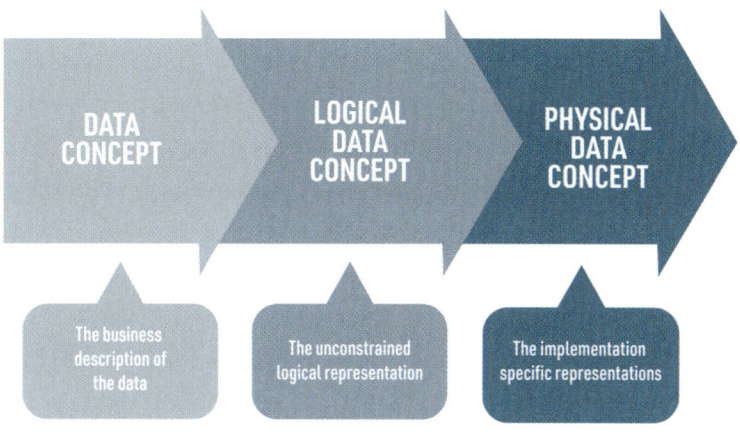

DATA CONCEPTS ARE ELABORATED AS A LOGICAL DATA MODEL, WHICH IS IMPLEMENTED AS ONE OR MORE PHYSICAL DATA MODELS

It is important to underscore that there are two distinct types of data models, as follows:

Logical Data Model (LDM): An abstract description of the data concept, unburdened by any physical constraints or optimizations, yet still of sufficient detail to accurately describe and disambiguate the data from other data concepts. It must be implementation agnostic.

Physical Data Model (PDM): An implementation-specific representation of the data once the LDM is manifested in a physical store of a specific type, such as a relational database. It may introduce additional metadata specific to the implementation or system requirements. There are likely to be multiple valid PDMs related to a single LDM.

INFORMATION ARCHITECTURE AT THE ENTERPRISE LEVEL

From an Enterprise Architecture perspective, Information Architecture's primary responsibility is to establish a taxonomy for your firm's core data concepts. This taxonomy describes a high-level representation of the data required by the business functions within a process. At this level the structure's details are not needed. Here, your goal is to create unambiguous descriptions that are easy for senior stakeholders and business owners to understand *within the context of the functions that consume or emit them*. It sounds straightforward, but in reality there will be duplicates and overlaps to reconcile. Consider a simple term such as "client." Some may consider this to be the individual they support (such as in retail banking), while others may consider it to be the institution (such as in wholesale banking). Creating an agreed-upon taxonomy, and perhaps leveraging a hierarchy to help organize it, will be both challenging and incredibly important.

At the Enterprise Level, it is also necessary to introduce an inventory system that registers all the physical assets that are used as data sources. This may include databases of varying types, file systems, programmatic interfaces, or APIs. This inventory will ensure that you can make accurate assessment of the data estate. It should label discovered data sources with the data concepts they contain, which will enable you to analyze your data estate and facilitate activities such as data lineage. In turn, this allows you to trace your firm's data assets at the data concept level as they transition across the enterprise. This will help you understand where data reconciliation may be required. This is critical when looking to resolve data quality issues.

As your comprehension of your data landscape evolves, you can further delineate your data sources, identifying those that should be considered your *Systems of Record* for a specific data concept. These are authoritative sources for that data concept, where maintenance activities such as creation, updating, and deletion are performed.

Ideally, there will be a very small number of Systems of Record for a specific data concept, with only one being ideal for things such as reference data. More often than not, multiples may be required. For example, there may be a need for a specific source for the same data concept for a particular country or product type.

However, minimizing the number of Systems of Record is important. That is not to say that you will not need a number of specific data sources to access the same data concept. Multiples may be required for performance and resilience reasons. These other sources should be considered as *Authorized Distributors* for a specific data concept. It is important to enforce that the Authorized Distributors do not mutate the data in any way; instead, they act as read-only sources.

You should also recognize that one physical source may be associated with more than one data concept. This complexity should be expected. Systems and applications will almost certainly consume more than one data concept to complete their activities. Moreover, to simplify Data Management, there will often be a consolidation of data concepts into a single physical source. When maintaining a single data source within an inventory entry, it's important to distinguish which data concepts are considered Systems of Record and which are Authorized Distributors.

Beyond the data concept, other metadata may be useful to associate with your data sources, such as the business owner (required by Data Governance) and the technical owner (required by Data Management).

INFORMATION ARCHITECTURE AT THE SOLUTIONS LEVEL

While data concepts help you establish a broad comprehension of your firm's data needs, they lack the precision required to design appropriate solutions and systems. Elaborating on these details is the responsibility of Solutions Architecture, and it is accomplished through the creation of LDMs. Data modeling is another area with an expansive corpus of knowledge. If you are not already familiar with it, I encourage you to immerse yourself.

When it comes to precisely defining what an LDM is responsible for, the following diagram represents a succinct representation of the core concepts. Each concept is important to understand in isolation and in relation to one another.

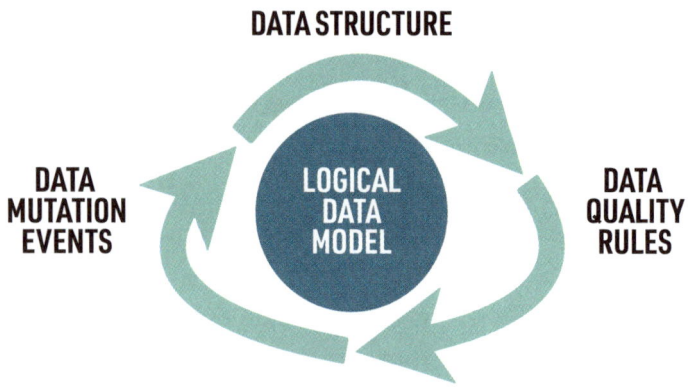

INTERDEPENDENT COMPONENTS OF A LOGICAL DATA MODEL

Data Structure: First, identify the actual data fields that describe the data concept. For a simple example of a *Person*, there may be fields such as *First Name, Last Name, Gender at Birth, Social Security Number*, and *Date of Birth* that collectively describe an *instance* of a person. Each data field may include metadata—other data that is present to describe the field, for example, whether the Date of Birth is a valid date.

Why do I refer to a "structure" instead of a "list of all the data fields"? Because rather than thinking of these as individual items forming the data, it is important to recognize that there may be relationships and interdependencies between them. If there are related fields, group them as a structure. Another important concept to remember is that one of the fields, or data structures, should provide unique values that help identify a specific instance of a person. In our example, this could be the Social Security Number—or if we have concerns about future reuse of Social Security Numbers, it could be the combination of Social Security Number and Last Name.

Data Quality Rules: Second, there must be rules that define the conditions required for individual data fields to be considered valid. For our Person example, we may want to specify that Gender at Birth is constrained to "Male," "Female," or "Intersex," or that Date of Birth may not be a date in the future and should be in the format MM/DD/YYYY.

These rules truly define the correctness of the data at hand. When you consider data quality rules, the usefulness of the previously defined data structure becomes clear. Invariably, a quality rule will depend on other attributes, such as "this attribute cannot be unpopulated if this other attribute has a value."

As another simple example, consider a different data concept: a simplistic *Trade* with fields such as *Security Identifier*, *Buy/Sell Indicator*, *Quantity*, and *Unit Price*. In this example there would also be a data quality rule stating that the Buy/Sell Indicator must have a value of either "Buy" or "Sell." However, there could be additional rules stating that if it is "Buy," there must be a positive Quantity, and if it is "Sell," then there must be a negative Quantity. In both instances, if Quantity is present, the Unit Price should have a positive value. Data quality rules also help validate the completeness of the data structures. When defining a data quality rule, it may become apparent that additional fields are required.

Data Mutation Events: Finally, we need to understand the events that will create or mutate the data in some way. The simplest events may be the creation, updating, or deletion of the data, but there can also be more complex business events specific to the data concept, such as *Book Trade* event for our *Trade* example. When this event occurs, the previously defined data quality rules would need to be validated.

Creating individual LDMs for each of your firm's required data concepts is an incredibly important architectural activity. It provides an unconstrained representation of what the data at your firm should be. It may be tempting to start by assessing your existing PDMs, but I do not recommend this. Yes, doing so can help build out your required data concepts, but your LDMs should be *independent of any implementation specifics*. It is important to be uninfluenced by what was created before.

This may feel like a complex and time-consuming activity; however, given they will be independent of any implementation specifics, they will not change significantly once they have been created. LDMs effectively define what "good data" looks like at your firm. As an unconstrained and idealistic model, comparing these new models to any existing ones will help greatly in assessing your firm's alignment to "good."

Defining the Data Structures

Many detailed resources exist to describe approaches on how to develop your data models, so I don't intend for this section to be a master class on data modeling techniques. However, it will be worthwhile to provide some basic techniques that should be useful to you.

At Oracle, we were taught *Entity-Relational* techniques for modeling data. This type of data modeling includes three basic components: Entities, Attributes, and Relationships. An Entity is analogous to the data concepts we discussed previously—that is, a description of a real-world entity. Attributes are the data fields that specify the entity. The new component here is the Relationship, which describes how different entities relate to one another.

In this way, the *Person* we described previously would be the entity, and its data fields, such as *First Name*, *Last Name*, *Gender at Birth*, and *Social Security Number*, would be the attributes. Let us consider a second entity, *Company*. A Person may work at a specific Company, so this would define a relationship of *Works At*.

These relationships are what make the Entity-Relationship model so powerful, as they promote data consistency and integrity. Understanding these relationships is fundamental to completing the LDM. Without doing so, you risk inflating any specific entity with extraneous data structures. In our example we *could* add attributes to the Person entity to represent their workplace, but doing so could create redundancy and imprecision. Many people would likely work at the same company, so the data would be repeated in many instances of a Person. Similarly, the Company may have its own unique relationships that would be nonsensical when connected to a specific Person.

In developing entities, we seek above all to *normalize* the data. We want to ensure that all attributes are relevant to an instance of the entity without repetition or redundancy. The simplest way to identify these relationships is through *verb analysis*. What does this mean? Consider your data concepts as nouns and describe the relationship between two data concepts using a verb. For example, let us consider a few basic data concepts: *Person*, *Company*, and *Address*. Consider the following relationships:

A Person **Works** at a Company

A Person **Lives** at an Address

A Company **Operates** from an Address

These relationships help delineate the data structures. It would be simple to include Address data structures in the definition of the Person, representing where they live and work. However, doing so, as previously mentioned, would create duplication and redundancy. Many people likely work at the same Company, and more than one person likely lives at the same Address. So by extracting these as entities and relationships, we *normalize* the data, eliminating redundant data from the data model.

INFORMATION ARCHITECTURE AT THE SOFTWARE LEVEL

LDMs provide a detailed, *unconstrained* view of the core data concepts that are required to support your firm's objectives. However, they are not operational data models. Until the data is materialized into physical assets—databases, reports, and file extracts—it has no intrinsic value to your firm or practical use. An operational representation of the data is required, and it must include all the *constraints* the process may introduce. This necessitates the development of a PDM.

The constraints that the PDM may introduce include additional enrichments, whether they are required to meet the nonfunctional requirements or to conform to requirements related to storage or transport technology mandates. For example, one requirement may be to include audit data. This would mandate the introduction of new fields to identify *who made changes to the data and when*. To improve performance, it may be beneficial to *denormalize* the data structures so that a single query returns all the required data. Information Architecture at the Software Architecture Level is responsible for developing appropriate PDMs based on the specific requirements that are to be met. It is important at the same time to understand the consequences of various trade-offs that come with departing from a pure, unadulterated logical model.

How you develop your PDMs will depend on specific nonfunctional requirement, the coding language being used, and the specific technologies that will be applied (as dictated by Technology Architecture). For example, leveraging the *Unified Modeling Language*[14] *(UML)* to develop an object-oriented class diagram may be appropriate for supporting the building of an application. Alternatively, Apache Avro[15] may be more suitable when defining the data models for data serialization between applications. There are a multitude of different approaches and products that could be applicable, so how you proceed will depend on what exactly you are trying to achieve. In all instances it is incredibly important to maintain a mapping back to the logical models, as in this way, the fidelity and consistency of all data models may be maintained.

A simple truth is, the closer your PDM aligns with the associated LDM and the more it leverages the least differing solutions for transport and storage, the less complicated your solution will be. The less reconciliation between data sources needed to demonstrate the consistency and quality of your data, the better.

CORE CONCEPT: REFERENCE AND MASTER DATA

There are two foundational data types that other data concepts will have a dependency on: *Reference* and *Master Data*. They are similar but subtly different, as explained below:

Reference Data: Usually aligned with external standards, it provides enrichment to other data concepts, such as ISO currency or country codes.

Master Data: Refers to enterprise-specific data definitions shared across various business processes of a firm, such as client or product.

Both Reference and Master Data are integral in defining the data concepts that your firm's business processes and associated functions will require. Identify these data concepts early, as the correctness and appropriateness of these data sources will substantially influence the overall data quality at your firm. It is also an area where consolidation and simplification should be comparatively straightforward.

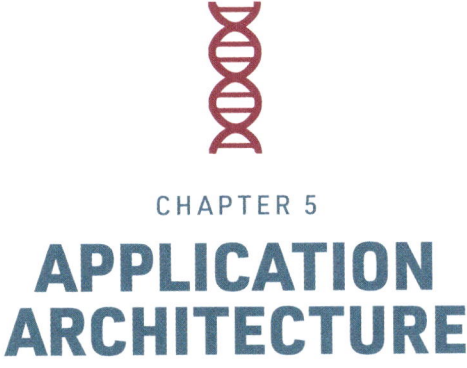

CHAPTER 5

APPLICATION ARCHITECTURE

Software is a great combination between artistry and engineering.

–BILL GATES

Application Architecture is an area where there is a broad and varied set of definitions about what it exactly is. Descriptions vary from it being "a structural map that provides a guide for how to assemble software applications"[16] to "the discipline that guides application design"[17] or "focuses on the design of applications."[18] While these definitions are all valid, they demonstrate the need for disambiguation, particularly with regard to the level of architecture at hand. Considering the discipline of Application Architecture at the levels of Enterprise, Solutions, and Software will help us make sense of these differing viewpoints.

Application Architecture lends itself to leverage one of the many robust frameworks and approaches that already exist across the industry. As such, this is not an area where I have felt the need to simplify or develop my own approach. I believe your approach to architecture will adapt based on several considerations, including what you are trying to achieve, the target deployment environment, the development tools and methodologies you are using, and the coding language and technology constraints at play. That said, it's worth discussing some of the basic considerations you should be aware of.

APPLICATION ARCHITECTURE AT THE ENTERPRISE LEVEL

Much like Information Architecture, from an Enterprise Architecture perspective, the responsibility of Application Architecture is fairly limited. It is primarily concerned with mapping application instances to the appropriate Business Architecture taxonomies, enabling the enterprise to be assessed and opportunities or risks to be identified to drive strategic investments. This does, however, identify the need for a key resource, an *Application Portfolio Management (APM)* tool to register your applications and enrich them with the necessary metadata.

Application Portfolio Management (APM)

This inventory is crucial to a number of governance activities, from operational risk management and business continuity planning to strategic investment governance. All instances of *functional* software products that your firm develops or *acquires* should be recorded. Although the name may suggest this is just for applications, all software components running in production, or planned to be, should be included. This includes all executable software components, such as microservices, web services, data integration, and databases.

Many of these components will be orchestrated and considered as a single "application." However, each will likely have dedicated responsibilities and development teams supporting them. Similarly, certain shared services or components may be utilized by more than one application. There may be a complex network of relationships between your components, and capturing this complexity is important for several reasons. At the most basic level, it allows you to identify interdependencies, which is essential for coordinating change and incident management activities. Before making changes, it is important to understand the scope of impact that the change may have. Similarly, when there is an incident, the dependencies can be analyzed to identify potential root causes.

All software components should be associated with the most precise enterprise taxonomy, from Business and Information Architecture, that describes their purpose. The application itself may exist to support a specific business process and may also leverage a specific service to fulfill a functional need. As described in the "Information Architecture" chapter, the various databases and stores will pertain to specific data concepts, and this should also be recorded. All this mapping within the APM supports the ability to track progress being made in Business Architecture and helps assess maturity and progress toward strategic objectives.

Remember, the APM stores details of each instance of a *functional* software product *running* in your production environment. It is important to recognize that there may be many instances of the same application, perhaps as a result of a resilience strategy or to create specific instances for a country or region. Additional metadata to identify this should be included, such as the country being supported or other details that account for why there are multiple instances.

I've already said that the software components your firm develops should also be recorded, and those *acquired* as third-party solutions or leveraged as managed services need to be too. When considering technology risk, business continuity, resilience, or even strategic investments, these third-party solutions are just as important to understand. Know upfront that they will almost certainly be opaque, meaning you may not necessarily understand how they were built, among other technical considerations. But if they support your business processes, it's critical to know their responsibilities, key contacts (internal and external), and any associated service-level agreements in place.

The APM will *not* be used to store details of the technology products and platforms your firm uses. Why not? Later, in the Technology Architecture section, we will discuss two other critical inventories that your firm should have in place: the IT Asset Management (ITAM) and Configuration Management Database (CMDB). I will not cover their details here; suffice it to say that one records the technology products in use, and the other tracks where software components (a.k.a. applications) are running. Within the APM, each component should have a relationship to any technology product it may leverage, as stored in the ITAM. Similarly, each running instance should have a relationship to the items stored in the CMDB.

This simple diagram helps explain these relationships:

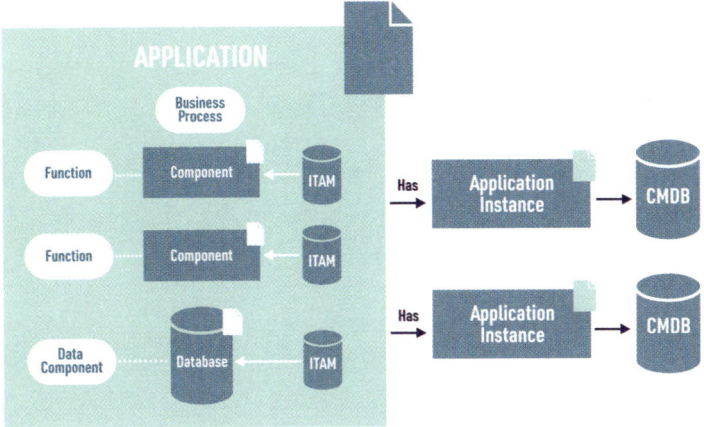

APPLICATION PORTFOLIO MANAGEMENT RELATIONSHIPS

From this we can infer the following relationships:

- The Application has an entry in the APM with specific details, such as the application's business and technical owner, recovery objectives, and status (e.g., whether it is under development or in production).

- The Application has an association with the business process it supports (derived as part of Business Architecture).

- The Application consists of an orchestration of one or more Components, both software and data stores.

- Each software Component has an association with the function it supports (also derived as part of Business Architecture).

APPLICATION ARCHITECTURE 65

- The data Component has an association with the data concepts it supports (derived as part of Information Architecture).

- All Components potentially leverage Technology Products stored in the ITAM repository.

- There is at least one—and potentially many—Application Instance(s) that are also entries in the APM. Specific details on the instances are recorded, such as country or region supported.

- Each Application Instance has an entry in the CMDB.

Many commercial APM products are available, often including ITAM and CMDB solutions. However, one free open-source project that provides a good introduction is Waltz,[19] a project within the *Fintech Open Source Foundation*,[20] an open source foundation that is "an independent setting to deliver software and standards that address common [Financial Service] industry challenges and drive innovation." It is highly customizable, allows you to build out the appropriate model for your organization, and provides comprehensive documentation and a demonstration example to help you on your way.

APPLICATION ARCHITECTURE AT THE SOLUTIONS LEVEL

The Solutions Architecture level requires an understanding of the whole system necessary to create a solution that addresses a specific problem. Rarely, if ever, does a single application provide the entire solution. There will be an interrelationship among different applications and services, as well as upstream and downstream dependencies that contribute to the overall solution.

Assess existing applications or services first, as they may fulfill part of the functional responsibility of the required solution, and then identify necessary data sources to provide the required data. Evaluating what already exists is extremely important. The more you can reuse existing solutions, the less complexity there will be. Application Architecture at the Solutions Level must consider all these factors and propose the most appropriate solution, and there may be more than one. It should also make use of insights and details from the various application mappings completed at the Enterprise Level.

When it comes to the actual tools and techniques you need to complete this activity, I do not have a strong bias. What is more important is that, regardless of the diagrammatic approach you take, it should show how the solution addresses the problem at hand, effectively communicate with the stakeholders, and provide enough detail for software architects to translate it into the necessary technical specifics.

APPLICATION ARCHITECTURE AT THE SOFTWARE LEVEL

Finally, at the Software Architecture level, the developer is required to consider how to construct the new applications that are required to meet the areas of functionality missing from the solution. They should also determine how it should best integrate with any existing applications or services that have been identified as being required. They can adopt a variety of design approaches, but one fundamental characteristic of effective design is to understand how best to employ *Software Architecture Patterns*.

Software Architecture Patterns

A pattern is a widely recognized approach to addressing a recurring design problem. Rather than laying out detailed design instructions, it provides the broad components and interactions necessary for implementation. Whether you have realized it or not, there is a strong likelihood that you've already made use of patterns, even if you have not recognized them as such.

Here are a few examples of some common design patterns:

Event-Driven Architecture Pattern: An *event* is a significant change in the state of a system or environment. An *Event-Driven Architecture* is one whereby an application or service detects and responds to a specific event or confluence of events. This is ideal when looking to create an extremely distributed and loosely coupled solution, as the *event producer* is unaware of the actions and intent of the *event consumer*. This type of architecture greatly simplifies horizontally scaling solutions, making them resilient to failures and allowing a number of parallel event consumers to work independently of one another. Amazon Web Services, whose services commonly produce or consume events, provides some concise documentation.[21]

Layered Architecture Pattern: When I started as a programmer, applications were predominantly built as large monoliths. Around the advent of the internet, a new approach, the *Layered* or *n-Tier Architecture*, arrived. This forced the software architect to separate the responsibilities of a solution into a number of distinct layers: *Presentation*, *Business*, and *Persistence*. This provided significant advantages, most of all by delineating responsibilities and allowing isolation between the layers. For example, the team working on building the presentation layer for a solution was distinct from the one building the services to encapsulate the business logic. So as not to show bias to any particular CSP, Microsoft Azure provides some useful documentation.[22]

Microservices Architecture Pattern: This is another pattern that helps structure a solution with loosely coupled components, a collection of services in this case. This promotes the benefits of component independence and scalability by decomposing an application into smaller components that can be independently developed to support specific functionality. Google Cloud Platform has some documentation that discusses this pattern.[23]

These are just three of a multitude of different architectural patterns. The main skill of the software architect is understanding the requirements well enough to apply the right one for the right purpose.

Building Applications

Applications and functional services will need to be designed, engineered, and ultimately deployed in an appropriate hosting environment. This must be done while adhering to all applicable technology and cybersecurity standards and adopting applicable development methodologies and tools (which will be determined as part of Technology Architecture).

I will not advocate for a particular development methodology, but I will emphasize some principles that I believe are important to consider when building solutions.

Build an early prototype: It doesn't matter how detailed the specification is. As soon as you commit code and create an early solution, the understanding of the real requirements quickly solidifies, for both you and the sponsor. By doing this, you can quickly resolve ambiguities and incorporate feedback.

Focus on the musts: Requirements tend to be prioritized as high, medium, or low, which I have always found to be somewhat ambiguous. Invariably, someone comes up with a higher priority, or something considered medium suddenly becomes critical. Instead, prioritize the requirements based on what *must* be completed for the first iteration to ensure the software is usable instead of focusing on what *should* be completed. These additional requirements can almost always be completed later. In this way, you will build what is often termed a *Minimum Viable Product*,[24] which is just a fancy way of saying "just the things that you really need to be functional and usable in the first instance."

Test early and test often: As you design your software, consider up front, what test assertions need to be validated for the solution to work as designed. With the advent of AI code assistance and products such as *GitHub Copilot*,[25] this is far less arduous than it used to be. Writing tests may at first feel counterintuitive, but it forces developers to design smaller, more focused components.

There are many excellent resources available to help here. When I was a "real" technologist, I found *The Pragmatic Programmer* by Andrew Hunt and David Thomas, particularly enlightening, but many more have since surfaced. Enjoy!

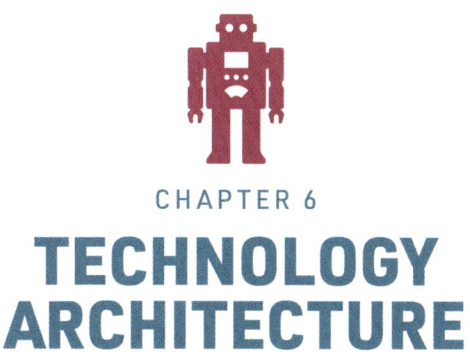

CHAPTER 6

TECHNOLOGY ARCHITECTURE

We are stuck with technology, when what we really want is just stuff that works.

—DOUGLAS ADAMS

There is a bit more consistency in the prevailing definitions of *Technology Architecture* compared with others we have discussed thus far. Just as Application Architecture describes the software applications that need to be designed and developed to solve a specific business problem, Technology Architecture is concerned with the fundamental technology components that comprise the infrastructure on which the applications will be deployed and executed. It provides a more concrete view of the mechanism by which this happens.

Traditionally, infrastructure has been considered synonymous with *hardware*, the physical platforms that the application would be hosted on, along with the associated operating system. But the purview of Technology Architecture is much broader than that.

Consider public cloud hyperscalers, such as Amazon Web Services or Microsoft Azure, where we no longer dictate the physical assets on which an application runs; instead, we configure infrastructural services to host that application. This can provide significant advantages in resiliency and scale, albeit only if your architecture's design factors these concerns into account.

As such, Technology Architecture must determine which infrastructure and platform-as-a-service solutions should be used to host its solutions. If, as the CTO, you also have responsibility for the development and operation of your firm's infrastructure, then it would also be your responsibility to engineer these services to meet your firm's standards.

Beyond infrastructure, Technology Architecture must also consider the foundational services that the application teams should or must leverage. Which database products should be used? Which messaging infrastructure? What standard software components, commercial or open source, should be incorporated into solutions to solve common business-agnostic problems, such as logging, authentication, or building the user interface?

TECHNOLOGY ARCHITECTURE AT THE ENTERPRISE LEVEL

At the Enterprise Architecture Level, Technology Architecture ensures that you are developing the applications on the right platforms and infrastructure solutions. As such, there needs to be a mechanism to easily identify the mandated solutions and, importantly—if not more importantly—the solutions that should *not* be used. To facilitate this, establish an IT Asset Management (ITAM) system to identify which products can be used.

The ITAM system is a foundational part of managing technology products across the enterprise. It should be *the* authoritative inventory system and should itemize the technology products in use while capturing sufficient details to ensure effective technology governance.

At the most basic level, the following information should be captured in the ITAM system:

Name and Description: At a minimum, the name of the product and a concise description are required, as names are not always self-explanatory.

Vendor, Make, and Model: The technical details of the product, including the vendor that supplied the product and other relevant specifications.

Financial and Contractual Information: While your firm may have dedicated procurement systems, capturing some basic financial and contractual details, such as contract renewal dates and cost centers being charged for the product, can help with proactive financial planning and strategy.

Licensing Details: Ensuring compliance with licensing restrictions is a critical aspect of technology product management. Again, this may be retained in a dedicated procurement system, but understanding any restrictions, license volumes, usage, and service-level agreements is key. Not doing so can result in significant financial penalties.

Type: A simple differentiation of the type of product, such as hardware, cloud service, or software. This can be as elaborate as you find useful.

Category: To ensure proactive management of the technology products in use at your firm, a category, such as database, networking, or server computing, is needed. By understanding which products are being utilized, you can eliminate the introduction of new products with duplicative capabilities, which will reduce costs and complexity. Of course, it is likely that you will require more than one product in the same category, whether as a result of different hosting approaches or nuanced features. In the end ensuring that this is a conscious decision is key.

Owner: Who is the internal expert responsible for future negotiations and best practices on the use of the product? If at all possible, elevating ownership to a category of products is desirable, as the person in charge will be incentivized to proactively manage an entire portfolio of related products.

It is likely that over the lifetime of a product, your firm will leverage a number of different versions of the same product. It is important to differentiate these versions, as there will be a lead time for you to review and approve new versions, which may need to be tested to validate new features. Regression testing, or repeatedly testing an application's features after updates or changes to ensure they still work as intended, may be needed to ensure compatibility with existing solutions. You will also want to deprecate or phase out existing versions of products in use, encouraging the use of the newer, up-to-date versions that address defects or known security flaws.

As such, for each product you should also capture **Version and Life Cycle Status**, or the life cycle for a specific version of a product, which could include stages such as planning, pilot, approved, phase out, and forbidden.

ITAM versus CMDB

There is another important inventory system that should not be confused with the ITAM: the Configuration Management Database (CMDB). Whereas the ITAM stores details about the products in use at your firm to enable effective governance and oversight, a CMDB stores information on the configuration details of specific instances of the products in use.

Entries stored in a CMDB are often termed *Configuration Items* (CIs), and there should be an entry for every piece of hardware or software in use at your firm, as each of these will require a specific configuration to operate securely and efficiently. There will be interdependencies between items that you must also capture. For example, an instance of server hardware from a vendor would require an entry. To actually be useful, this would necessitate installing an operating system on it, which would also require an entry. Just as importantly, the relationship between these two CIs should be memorialized, as this represents the actual solution: two CIs, and likely many others, working in concert.

The CMDB is a critical inventory that needs to accurately reflect the status of all CIs at all times. It will be integral to a number of core technology operational processes, including change, incident, and problem management. It is important that all configuration changes are reflected as and when they are made. For example, if there is an incident, the CMDB should be able to identify where recent changes have been made that may have caused or contributed to that incident. Similarly, when changes are being made, the interdependencies can be analyzed to understand the scope of the items that may be affected. A well-maintained and accurate CMDB is critical to these processes operating effectively.

TECHNOLOGY ARCHITECTURE AT THE SOLUTIONS LEVEL

Again, rarely, if ever, does a single technology product provide all the capabilities required to effectively support an application in isolation. Technology Architecture at the Solutions Level is where different products are selected to work together to provide a comprehensive solution. If we consider a simple infrastructural service, such as a relational database, we may at first think that by merely selecting an appropriate database product, we would provide an appropriate solution.

While the database product is most certainly *key* to providing that capability, a number of other considerations must be made. On what platform will it be hosted? How will usage be monitored? How will you protect the data, provide archival capabilities, and prevent data loss? If we plan to provide a resilient platform for our applications, the database solution must reflect all these considerations and more. While minimizing the different products and vendors required should certainly be an objective, know that, without a doubt, different products will need to be carefully coordinated and integrated into your final solution.

I have found it useful to focus on understanding the *interdependencies* between capabilities and to cleanly delineate the responsibilities for providing appropriate solutions. This minimizes the likelihood of duplication and redundancy. For example, if one group is responsible for providing compute solutions for the whole firm, they can focus on robust, resilient, and secure compute solutions. If a different group is responsible for database solutions, they would be a consumer of the compute solutions. As such, their requirements must be met, but they may not have the autonomy to create alternative compute solutions. This schema offers the best chance of reuse, concentration, and consistent technology solutions.

Here are a few delineations of technology solutions that I have found useful in this regard:

Network: The various solutions that provide all aspects of network connectivity, including local and wide area networks, wireless and mobile solutions, high-speed local networks for storage solutions, and internet connections.

Storage: The underlying file, block, and object stores that support other solutions, provide protection against data loss and ransomware, facilitate backup and retrieval, and enable data caching.

Compute: The generic term for the various services that support all types of computational workloads. This may include physical and virtual machines, serverless solutions (that obfuscate the underlying hardware), mainframe, or even quantum computers.

Database: The opinionated storage solutions, which will almost certainly depend on the previously listed technology solutions, to provide various database solutions. This may include relational, graph, objective, and NoSQL solutions.

End User: Simply put, the things that the personnel at your firm will use to do anything. This includes laptops, mobile solutions, and personal computers, each of which needs to be managed and secured, as well as core infrastructure components such as video conferencing, telephony, and email.

Some of you may think that I have erroneously omitted cloud from the list, but this is deliberate. I consider cloud to merely be a hosting choice. Regardless of whether the solution is based in an in-house private data center or provided by a cloud service provider (CSP), the technology solutions should be the accountability of the same group. This creates an incentive to ensure that the solutions offered meet all requirements and standards, regardless of the hosting choice.

In my experience, where there has been a dedicated group accountable for cloud, they must replicate solutions for all the other groups listed. This introduces a significant risk for a potential divergence of capability, standards, and approach. In my experience this type of artificial "competition" for internal consumption rarely results in positive outcomes. The most complex activity—moving from an existing in-house hosted solution to the cloud—is often not prioritized appropriately.

There is one last group of technology solutions that needs to be included: those related to the tools and services required to design and develop the applications that your firm requires. These **Application Services** consist of a multitude of disparate technology solutions, from collaboration tools to project management software, code development environments, and software scanning solutions. Each needs to be developed, operated, and supported consistently with any other critical production services. Should any of these application services fail, loss of productivity is just the beginning. If there are any other technology-related incidents that require coding intervention during an outage, the facilities to do so would not be available, which poses an enormous risk.

Another nuance of application services is ensuring that they enforce standards through connectivity to both the ITAM and

CMDB solutions. The ITAM can provide sufficient details on the technology products that should and should not be used, so preventative controls can be established and enforced. Similarly, when deploying applications and services into the production environment, these development pipelines can update the CMDB, ensuring that there are timely and accurate automated updates. These both manifest one of the core CTO objectives that I mentioned earlier: "Codify Standards and Controls."

TECHNOLOGY ARCHITECTURE AT THE SOFTWARE LEVEL

Once your different technology groups determine precisely what's needed, this level is where you actually engineer and deliver specific solutions. In doing so, you must follow the same technology and cybersecurity standards that the Application developers had to adhere to before you. It sounds obvious, but unfortunately, it is not always the case. I've seen it occur in myriad ways: source code for the development of infrastructure services has not always been stored in firm-sanctioned code repositories, change management processes have not always been ardently followed, and solutions have not been sufficiently engineered and tested. As a consequence, unintended changes reduce or remove functionality, and solutions become less effective over time. Wholly avoidable issues and incidents invariably result.

It is incredibly important to engineer infrastructure services with rigor, diligence, and adherence to technology and cybersecurity standards. Because a multitude of different applications that potentially support a number of business processes may all depend on the same infrastructure, the blast radius caused by defects and incidents can be huge.

While Application Architecture at this level is concerned with building and deploying an application or service, Technology Architecture's focus is on providing the appropriate infrastructure to deploy the application. This includes ensuring that it is successfully integrated with other components and applications.

Your initial instinct may be to think, *This still sounds like the responsibility of Application Architecture. Surely they must determine which other applications and services they need to connect to?* That is absolutely true. However, at the Software Level of Technology Architecture, you actually decide on the design of the solution, whether that means determining the network boundaries for the solution, the necessary communication protocols to be used, firewall rules to apply, or the specific hardware and associated software to use. To do all this, the integration and deployment architectures delivered must be specific to the Application solution deployed into production. At this level, similar to other disciplines, there are many valid approaches to take in developing integration and deployment diagrams. UML provides a specific structural diagram: the *Deployment Diagram*.[26] It provides details of the interactions and dependencies between the software components and the necessary hardware required during execution. It focuses solely on the configuration and dependencies that are needed at run time. It is a powerful representation, as it surfaces all dependencies, which can be particularly useful when considering any systemic weaknesses, cybersecurity or otherwise, that need to be addressed. This is an area where the form is less important than the function. You can determine the most appropriate mechanism to create your deployment diagrams, but please be certain to create them.

CHAPTER 7

SECURITY ARCHITECTURE

It takes twenty years to build a reputation and few minutes of cyber-incident to ruin it.
—STÉPHANE NAPPO

Establishing appropriate security and cyber resilience for your firm will require dedicated specialist expertise. As the CTO, you will partner with your firm's chief information security officer (CISO) rather than assuming sole responsibility for this discipline. Describing the various responsibilities of a CISO in detail would require another book, as their purview extends well beyond Security Architecture. This includes defining the security strategy for the firm, establishing and monitoring the security risk appetite, and potentially engineering the end-to-end security services to adopt. Given the increasingly sophisticated threats to security by bad actors, their most crucial responsibility may be ensuring that the evolving security and cyber threat landscape is well understood and appropriately mitigated.

I will not cover these CISO activities in detail here, but I will describe how they intersect with the holistic architecture activities under the remit of the CTO. It is critical that Security Architecture and Engineering is fully integrated into the overall technology processes. It cannot be an afterthought or an add-on. If it is, it will create weaknesses and vulnerabilities that nefarious actors will look to exploit.

SECURITY ARCHITECTURE AT THE ENTERPRISE LEVEL

Security must be a first-class consideration when planning and designing solutions. It greatly influences the overall technical solution and, importantly, the associated costs. Neglecting to prioritize security will, at best, create potential weaknesses and, at worst, result in an insecure and vulnerable solution.

This process begins with understanding the maturity of your firm's security capabilities. Though this is not a CTO's responsibility, I would strongly recommend investing the time to understand these capabilities and the cybersecurity risks that they address. Every organization is different, with business capabilities specific to their objectives, but the risks that they need to mitigate and desirable cybersecurity outcomes are fundamentally the same.

The *National Institute of Standards and Technology (NIST)* provides a *Cybersecurity Framework (CSF) 2.0*,[27] which was "designed to help organizations of all sizes and sectors—including industry, government, academia, and nonprofit—to manage and reduce their cybersecurity risks." This is not a prescriptive framework; instead, it suggests how to *address* security risks. It proposes *organizational profiles*, which help organizations compare where they are versus where they want or need to be. This is fundamental to the framework and a key aspect of Security Architecture at the Enterprise Level. As always, understanding a desirable *target state* and the gap to where your firm currently operates, or its *current state*, is paramount. As with the other disciplines, a high-level cybersecurity *taxonomy* of outcomes is at its core. Appendix A of CSF 2.0 describes the *CSF Core*, which outlines a hierarchy of *Functions*, *Categories*, and *Subcategories* necessary to create one or more organizational profiles.

To provide a summary and context, the following are the six core functions and their rationales:

> **Govern:** The set of overarching outcomes that help inform an organization on what they need to establish to ensure effective security risk management and oversight of the other functions.
>
> **Identify:** Encapsulates the outcomes to understand an organization's current assets—such as hardware, software, and applications—and their associated suppliers. It also includes the identification of opportunities to improve security policies and standards (although I personally feel that this should be part of Govern). Risk assessment is also included to ensure that those assets that represent the greatest risk can be prioritized.
>
> **Protect:** The ability to secure and safeguard assets from known security risks, recognizing that different types of assets may necessitate different risk mitigations.
>
> **Detect:** Outcomes to help ensure timely detection and accurate assessment of anomalies or indicators of potential compromise.

Respond: Actions taken once a potential security breach has been detected. This is similar but distinct from the related technology process, as it includes security incident management and related root cause analysis.

Recover: Ensures a timely restoration of operations after a security incident and the associated communication plan depending on the severity of compromise.

Within each of these functions are specific Categories. For reference, I have included them in the following table. The *NIST Cybersecurity Framework 2.0 Reference Tool*[28] provides expanded details, including Subcategories.

Function	Category
GOVERN	Organizational Context
	Risk Management Strategy
	Roles, Responsibilities, and Authorities
	Policy
	Oversight
	Cybersecurity Supply Chain Risk Management
IDENTITY	Asset Management
	Risk Management
	Improvement
PROTECT	Identity Management, Authentication, and Access Control
	Awareness and Training
	Data Security
	Platform Security
	Technology Infrastructure Resilience
DETECT	Continuous Monitoring
	Adverse Event Analysis
RESPOND	Incident Management
	Incident Analysis
	Incident Response Reporting and Communication
	Incident Mitigation
RECOVER	Incident Recover Plan Execution
	Incident Recover Communication

CSF 2.0 CORE FUNCTION AND CATEGORY NAMES AND IDENTITIES

SECURITY ARCHITECTURE

Your CISO will use this taxonomy to build out assessments of current capabilities and levels of maturity, creating the organizational profiles that your firm requires. Within the *Govern* function, the CISO will develop appropriate cybersecurity policies, standards, and necessary oversight for the remaining functions—much like how you, as the CTO, will develop the technology equivalents.

I hope it is apparent from the table that there is an obvious intersection with technology activities. The *Identity Asset Management* wholly relies on the ITAM and CMDB inventory systems outlined in the Technology Architecture discipline. It is imperative that there is a single source of truth for IT Assets, driving both technology and cybersecurity processes and risk management.

The cybersecurity services developed as part of the *Protect* function must also be seamlessly integrated into the technology platforms and services you develop to provide core infrastructural services. The overall resilience of your infrastructure would be evaluated as part of the *Technology Infrastructure Resilience* assessment but through a cybersecurity lens.

As part of Security Architecture at the Enterprise Level, the CISO will be responsible for defining the necessary cybersecurity policies and standards, along with the supporting capabilities and security services that your organization will require. This will ensure that cybersecurity risks are identified and managed. But for there to be holistic success for your firm, there must be cooperation and comprehension between the CISO and CTO on who is accountable for what. The CTO must adopt the cybersecurity services defined by the CISO, the CISO must consume and leverage the technology services defined and delivered by the CTO, and both must respect and adhere to the policies and standards that each produces.

SECURITY ARCHITECTURE AT THE SOLUTIONS LEVEL

Much like Technology Architecture, Security Architecture at the Solutions Level is concerned with defining the necessary cybersecurity solutions to create and leverage. These solutions broadly align with the previously discussed technology service delineations: *Network*, *Storage*, *Compute*, *Database*, *End User*, and *Application Service*. While the industry groups these solutions in various ways, I consider cybersecurity services as follows:

Network Security: As the first line of defense, network security services such as firewalls and transport encryption *protect* the network, whereby intrusion detection systems help to *detect* nefarious or abnormal activities that may indicate security breaches.

Information Security: This involves protecting data integrity and availability, whether as part of an underlying storage or database service. It includes data encryption, access controls, and archive and retrieval services.

Application Security: As developers create code, it is critical that they adhere to and enforce secure coding standards through the use of code scanning tools. Introducing weak or inherently insecure code into production represents a significant cybersecurity risk. With the prevalence of applications leveraging third-party or open-source software packages, the "software supply chain" must be evidenced to be secure and trusted. There have been several high-profile software supply chain attacks,[29] and all signs indicate that this will continue to be a significant focus for hackers.

Infrastructure Security: I have seen this termed "cloud security," and it is fair to say that the public cloud does present some distinct security challenges, given that the infrastructure is being operated by a third party (often termed the shared responsibility model[30]). Yet all infrastructure, whether hosted in the public cloud or internally in private data centers, must have appropriate preventative and detective controls in place to safeguard it. Some solutions will be wholly hosted on the public cloud, while others will reside entirely within internal data centers. However, for the foreseeable future, large enterprises will need to secure solutions that span both.

Endpoint Security: I have seen this termed "mobile security," but I feel that term is a subset of endpoint security. The most common points of cyberattacks are the devices used by end users, such as laptops, mobile phones, tablets, desktop computers, and even servers. These must be secured and carefully monitored to detect potential security breaches.

Security Services: Finally, dedicated security services are essential, such as identity and access management and the logging and monitoring of security events. The latter may share technology solutions with other logging and monitoring services, but security data is often more sensitive, requiring stringent protection.

To implement appropriate solutions, there must be close coordination between the Security and Technology Solutions Architects. Security is nonnegotiable and must be applied to both the Application and Technology solutions. When security services are developed in isolation, they risk adversely affecting technology solutions.

Far too often I have seen Security Solutions that are essentially a smorgasbord of security products cobbled together under a loose rubric of "more is better." In these instances companies acquire multiple products, each of which offers a multitude of security features that often overlap in functionality and protection. A misunderstanding of how everything works and the exact protection provided creates an artificial sense of safety. This approach risks conflicts between products or, worse still, gaps in functionality. If the products are poorly engineered and *integrated*, the entire security posture will be ineffective or inefficient, which will lead to brittle solutions at best.

I've also seen security measures have adverse functional or nonfunctional impacts on the underlying technology services being secured. At one firm, multiple security solutions were installed to protect the endpoint desktop. The net result of all these products running on the desktop, doing similar things in different ways, resulted in terrible performance, slowed applications, and much consternation. We resolved the issue by *designing* the necessary security solution to monitor and protect the endpoint, then determined the appropriate security product to meet our needs.

So how do we effectively determine the security requirements? By creating *threat models*.

Threat Modeling

When considering cybersecurity risks, it's useful to think about the threats to mitigate to reduce those risks. When considering technology services, applications, or even business processes, a threat model provides a structural representation identifying where there are potential weaknesses and where an action can be taken to address or mitigate the threat.

A threat model typically consists of the following:

- A description of the model's subject, including a diagram or model that details the core components and associated data flows, which provides the boundaries or scope of what is being modeled.

- Identification of potential vulnerabilities or weaknesses in the model that could be exploited.

- The countermeasures or controls that should be introduced to reduce or eradicate the weakness. A single threat may require multiple controls working in concert to address it, and a single control may mitigate more than one threat.

Once your threat model is complete, an assessment can be made on how best to *implement* the necessary controls to secure the model's objective. The model can clarify the level of risk, the likelihood of exploitation, and how to prioritize remediation. You may also take other countermeasures outside the system into account as well.

It is important to note, though, that any threat model represents only *the threats known at the specific time that it was modeled*. Periodic validation is necessary, especially if there is a significant change. The threat landscape is ever evolving. Bad actors are constantly developing new exploits and approaches, and many will require new controls. Similarly, the threat model's subject, whether an application or technology service, is very likely to be modified and enhanced over time to introduce new features and capabilities. These may also introduce new weaknesses and vulnerabilities to address.

There are many cybersecurity resources available, but one that is particularly useful when considering threats is the *MITRE Adversarial Tactics, Techniques, & Common Knowledge (ATT&CK®)*.[31] This comprehensive resource of tactics and techniques is widely used in the cybersecurity industry to understand the threats that adversaries may use to exploit systems. It is open and available to any person or organization to use at no charge.[32]

Controls

When considering the necessary controls to introduce, it is useful to recognize that they will most likely fall into one of the following three categories:

Preventative Controls: These controls proactively block a weakness. They most commonly manifest in the configuration of a service, ensuring only the necessary features have been enabled. For example, perhaps a solution hosted in the public cloud requires the use of a file store. Assuming the application only uses this internally, the service should be configured to ensure that it is does not provide public access. With the *AWS S3 Service*, this is as straightforward as enabling the *Block Public Access*[33] feature.

Detective Controls: These controls detect, log, and notify security incidents that have occurred. In our simple file store example, if the service's configuration were to change to enable public access, this would result in a potential breach notification to the security operations center.

Corrective Controls (a.k.a. Responsive Controls): These controls attempt to automatically remedy potential breaches as they occur. To continue with our previous example, once public access had been enabled, a security monitoring agent could reset the configuration to the appropriate state. The same monitoring agent could also automatically quarantine the service in the face of repeated attempts to compromise it.

Consider each of these control types when looking to address potential threats and weaknesses. In line with my core objective of *Codify Standards and Controls*, I strongly endorse applying the controls programmatically whenever possible.

SECURITY ARCHITECTURE AT THE SOFTWARE LEVEL

At the Software Level, Security Architecture predominantly focuses on implementing security standards and best practices that must be adhered to. Again, NIST provides assistance here with their *Secure Software Development Framework*.[34] It provides a core set of high-level secure software development practices that can be integrated into the Application Architecture Software Development practices. While there are a number of best practices to follow, the most critical is ensuring that software is *secure by design*. This can result in longer development time frames, but neglecting security at the onset of developing software can create a false economy. As a CTO, I did not want to encounter the repercussions of an avoidable security breach resulting from poorly designed software.

Any necessary security services, even if functionally different, should be developed in tandem with the development of any other application or technology services. All should be developed following the latest technology and cybersecurity standards, hosted on your firm's infrastructure services, and governed in accordance with the processes and oversight that we will cover next.

PART II
GOVERNANCE

CHAPTER 8
ARCHITECTURE GOVERNANCE

*Don't write so that you can be understood,
write so that you can't be misunderstood.*
–WILLIAM HOWARD TAFT

Central to the role of the CTO is establishing and operating effective governance processes for all architectural and engineering activities. This is unlikely to be isolated from other existing corporate governance forums but rather subordinate to them. So initially, it is important to assess the existing governance forums to determine which should delegate the authority for architectural and engineering oversight.

In the chapter "Defining Architecture," the five architecture disciplines and three levels were introduced. These provide concise boundaries for both governance committees and the associated policies, standards, procedures, and architecture review processes. Before we delve into that, let's discuss some of the core tenets of effective governance.

GOVERNANCE PRINCIPLES

Regardless of the specific governance approach you adopt, I recommend adhering to the following core governance principles:

Ensure Unambiguous Accountability

For governance to be effective, there must be an understanding and acceptance of who truly has the authority *and* accountability to make specific governance decisions. Clarity on the delineation of responsibilities is crucial, and you must eliminate gray areas where more than one group potentially believes they have accountability for an activity or, even worse, doesn't have accountability when they should. Otherwise, it's easy for accidental or willful confusion to arise and spread across the organization. To eradicate ambiguity, governance forums should publish a clear charter through a document that lays out the committee's objectives, authority, and processes.

Ensure Transparency and Inclusion

Once you know who is accountable, it is important that the accountable owner's decisions and outcomes are readily available and easy to comprehend. Transparency can garner a great deal of trust in terms of the drivers and constraints that were considered ahead of making important decisions. Transparency promotes greater comprehension of the reasoning behind eventual outcomes, as well as acceptance of the outcome itself.

Ensure Competency

Too often, when I have seen governance forums fail, it is due to participants lacking credible competency. If current practitioners lack appropriate skills, the decisions they make are unsurprisingly rarely fit for purpose and lead to organizational reluctance or rejection. Conversely, if there is respect for those making the decisions and their expertise and competency are unquestioned, a stronger likelihood of acceptance tends to follow. Ensuring the appropriate competency of the participants can also improve the governance forum's "cachet," as it becomes recognized as an expert group for which membership is aspirational.

Ensure Attendance, Not Delegation

Participants must have sufficient capacity to be able to commit to the level of effort and engagement that the governance activities dictate. Where they don't, there is a tendency to delegate to others, which rarely is successful. Delegation can introduce ambiguity in accountability—and potentially a lack of appropriate competency—and may also set a precedent that delegation is acceptable, so that it invariably happens again.

Ensure Responsiveness

Good governance requires timely completion of actions. If not, governance processes can be perceived as inefficient and bureaucratic. There will always be some overhead in operating governance activities, but responsiveness, transparency, and competency usually promote timely engagement by those being governed.

GOVERNANCE FORUMS

At the most basic level, you will need to establish governance forums where there is a risk that needs to be addressed, which may be a process- or domain-specific risk. Governance forums are established to help control that risk, to ensure appropriate policies, standards, and procedures are in place, and to provide appropriate levels of supervision that promote effective operational management.

I recommend creating a charter for each governance forum. At a minimum this will provide the following details, recognizing that the specific risk being managed may introduce its own set of details:

- The *purpose and objectives* of the governance forum, including the scope of impact and influence the group has.

- The *membership*, including details on standing members, voting members, and guest contributors.

- The *operational cadence and procedures* that will be followed, including the frequency of assembly, whether a quorum is required, and details on the publication and approval of agendas and minutes.

- The *escalation procedures* to follow, detailing bodies from which the forum receives its authority.

- The *responsibilities* of the forum, including any policies, standards, and procedures that it is accountable for.

- The *key metrics and surveillance procedures* for which the forum is responsible.

One item worth reiterating is the importance of identifying where the governance forum receives its authority. Why is this group empowered to oversee this particular risk? If there is not an appropriate sponsoring group or forum—whether that is a senior executive group, the board, or even another governance forum—it will undermine credibility and the possibility of success.

POLICIES, STANDARDS, AND PROCEDURES

Throughout this book you may have noticed a recurring theme on the importance of both transparency and unambiguous accountability. To achieve them, you must establish appropriate policies, standards, and procedures. The importance of understanding the purpose of these interrelated yet distinct documents cannot be understated.

First and foremost, **Policy** documents provide a set of statements that articulate decisions made by a governing body to mitigate a specific set of risks and perhaps improve operations. Policies also encapsulate *why* an organization should do something.

Subordinate to the policy are one or more related **Standards**. These are actions that should support the realization of the policy intentions. Standards encapsulate *what* an organization should do to evidence adherence to the related policy.

Finally, the **Procedure** document relates to one or more standards and outlines the specific operational activities and tools that should be followed and maintained to adhere to the controls and, by extension, the standard itself. Procedures encapsulate the mechanics of *how* an organization should do something.

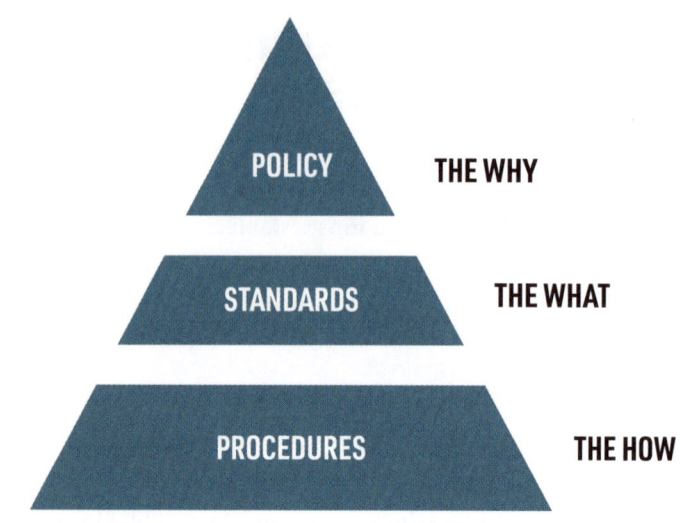

THE POLICY, STANDARDS, AND PROCEDURES PYRAMID OF RESPONSIBLITIES

The distinction between policies, standards, and procedures should be apparent. They form a clear hierarchy. The policy is the foundation and describes the organization's expectations. A set of standards provides details regarding what needs to occur. Finally, the specific implementation details are codified in the procedures. In sum, they provide the policy framework that an organization requires for effective governance.

Because they represent the overarching tenets that the organization is trying to achieve, policies are unlikely to change very often once they are established. The most common reason for making policy changes is significant shifts in the regulatory environment in which an organization operates, or appreciable changes to the strategies or strategic objectives. Standards are also relatively fixed: what your firm is trying to achieve is unlikely to change, even if how that should be achieved evolves.

Procedures, on the other hand, are quite likely to be

susceptible to change over time, as they should be continually improved. A procedure may initially describe a set of controls that rely on "trust and verify" activities, in which one actor completes an activity, while a second independent verifier confirms the efficacy and completeness of the action. This type of control may be acceptable but is not particularly robust, given its reliance on fallible human beings.

Over time you can introduce tools that provide preventative controls, whereby a system or tool codifies the controls and enforces the correct control behavior. This is a far more robust control implementation. However, what the control evidences—adherence to the standard—will not change.

Deviations from Policies, Standards, and Procedures

While deviations from an established policy, standard, or procedure do occur, it is not often. The reasons for why and when they do vary, but it is usually to address some greater issue or risk than that which is perceived in a breach. In these instances a suitable authority, including the owner of the standard being breached, must thoroughly review the situation to ensure that the breach is indeed merited. Take note of the *risk exception* and include details on what exactly the deviation is, why it can be deemed acceptable, and how long the exception is valid. In addition, a detailed *plan of action* should be associated with the risk exception to explain the actions that will take place to return to compliance and the timeline for doing so.

Curate Standards and Best Practices Developed by Practitioners

Establish one other useful concept: codifying the best practices that technology staff currently use. Know that this will not form part of the overall governance structure you need to establish and that these practices may not necessarily align with specific policies and standards. But by recognizing and identifying the best of them, you can create a strong basis for developing solid operational procedures. When your procedures are based on established, ongoing practices, they will not succumb to pitfall of cultural malaise, skepticism, and rejection.

ALIGNING GOVERNANCE WITH ARCHITECTURE DISCIPLINES

As previously described when introducing the five disciplines of architecture, each discipline requires distinct areas of expertise and focus. As such, it is beneficial to establish dedicated governance accountabilities—for the development and oversight of appropriate policies, standards, and procedures—aligned with these disciplines. To be truly effective, there must be an appreciation of the interdependencies that may exist between the disciplines, and it is important that accountabilities are clearly distinguished and that conflict resolution occurs promptly.

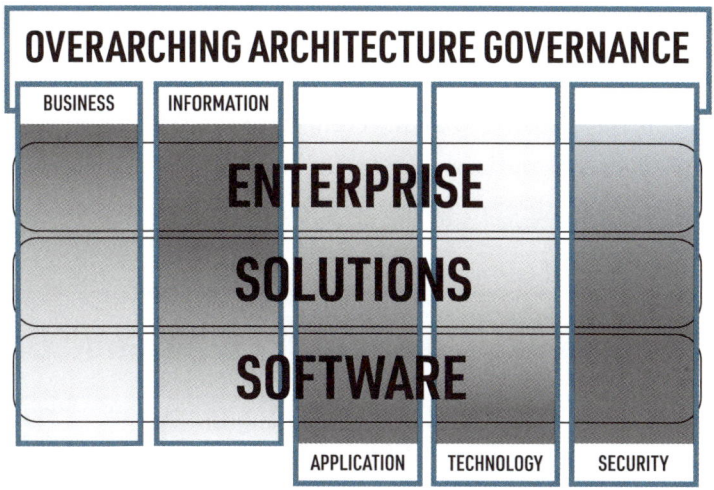

ARCHITECTURE GOVERNANCE WITH DISCIPLINE OWNERSHIP

To this end, an overarching architecture governance forum is required, with participation from senior representatives of the discipline-specific areas. I won't dictate exactly how this should be organized. I do recommend that each discipline elect a primary and a delegate representative who can vote on behalf of their discipline and that, for quorum, all areas must be represented by either the primary or delegate.

In practice, there is an optimization to this structure that can be beneficial. Although each discipline is distinct in its requirements, the Application Architecture discipline is the primary area where the other disciplines effectively come together. When developing an application, you must consider the security requirements, the functions that the application will fulfill, the data that it will consume or produce, and even the technology products and platforms that it will leverage and operate on. All architectural requirements physically manifest in the creation of the software asset, the application. Though there will be specific architectural requirements from a governance perspective, this is where the different disciplines will meet and where any ambiguity or conflict must be resolved. As such, the overarching architecture governance forum can also act as the owner and arbitrator for the Application Discipline, the "T-shaped" architecture governance model.

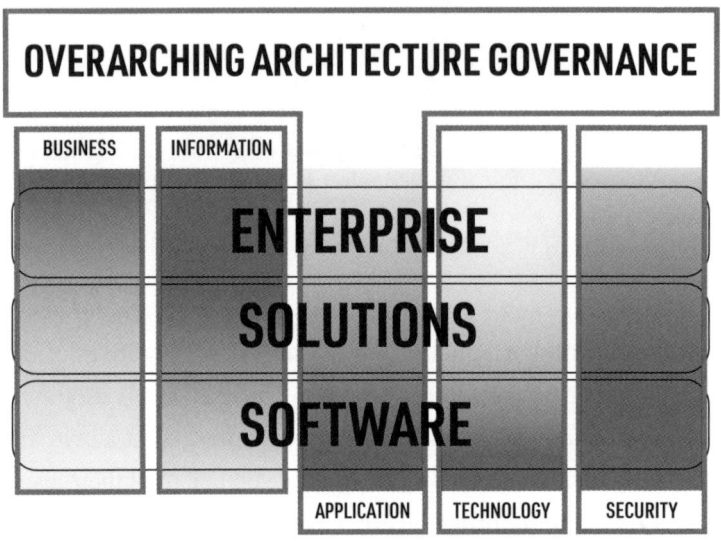

"T-SHAPED" ARCHITECTURE GOVERNANCE

ALIGNING GOVERNANCE WITH ARCHITECTURE LEVELS

As important as it is to ensure appropriate governance for each discipline of architecture, it is as important to ensure the appropriateness of the execution of architecture activities between the levels of architecture. In practice, this principally means that as strategies are developed, appropriate solutions are designed, and ultimately, the software products delivered to implement those solutions are "fit for purpose" and functionally correct. One mechanism to enforce this is to introduce review processes or "tollgates" that validate the efficacy of the *design, build,* and *deployment* of solutions.

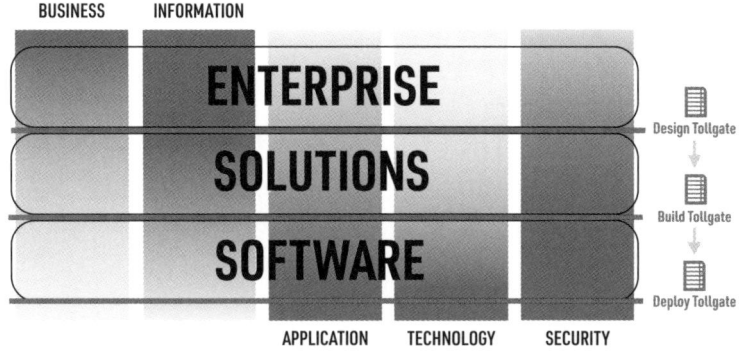

REVIEW TOLLGATES WHEN MOVING BETWEEN THE LEVELS OF ARCHITECTURE.

As we consider these tollgates and their likely alignment to development procedures, regardless of methodology adopted, we should recognize that activities explode as we move through the Enterprise, Solutions, and Software Levels.

Consider a situation where, at the Enterprise Level, you need to create a new business capability. This may require accomplishing a number of Solutions before considering that capability complete. Each Solution may then require the delivery of several Software assets for it to meet its functional requirements.

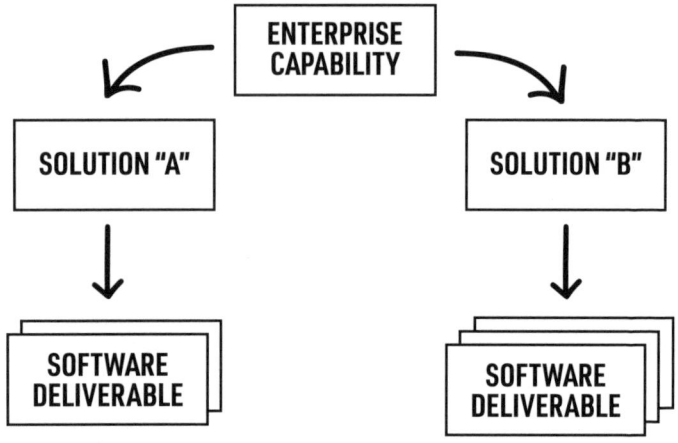

ENTERPRISE SOLUTION

As such, an inheritance will exist between the architecture tollgates. Once an Enterprise initiative has been approved, more than one solution may be permitted, with each solution requiring more than one software deployment to production to complete. It should not be necessary to revisit a prior approved tollgate, unless there has been a significant departure from the original intention and approved design.

In establishing review tollgates, try to ensure that the processes you introduce are synergistic with the existing design and development process.

Ideally, it should improve the process and be recognized as of value by its practitioners. If that is not achievable, it should not be seen as detrimental or an impediment to productivity. As silly as this sounds, I have too often observed the introduction of bureaucratic and ineffective solutions, where the very substance of the review is ill-suited and ineffective. Ironically, these reviews often can be easily validated as having taken place, an emphasis of audit or regulatory reviews, but that does not mean they were effective. It sounds obvious, but reviews should *add* value.

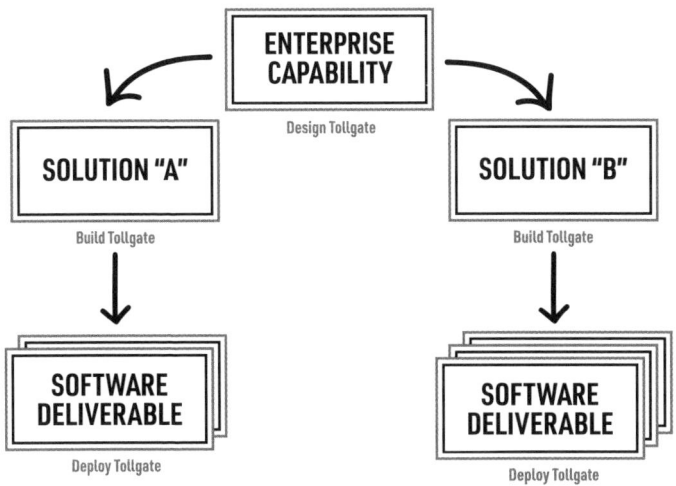

INHERITANCE OF PRIOR APPROVALS

Ideally, you should also automate the architecture review process as much as possible—it should be embedded in tooling and development pipelines. Given the variations of technology and adoptable processes, this is very difficult to achieve, but it should remain the ultimate objective nevertheless. A highly codified process that's integrated into the tooling being used for other purposes will significantly minimize disruption.

Architecture Significance Assessment

Any medium to large enterprise will have a significant number of development activities in flight at any one time, all of which must be considered and assessed as part of your architecture review process. Recognize that the level of rigor to apply will vary depending on the complexity or risks associated with the activity. For example, an activity that introduces a completely new system that addresses a business-critical capability will require significantly more attention and focus than a small functional enhancement to an existing asset. Even so, both should be subject to the architecture review process because even small changes can introduce risk or failures.

The first phase of an architecture review process is to assess the *architectural significance* of an activity. This should form part of the first design tollgate and can be achieved in a number of different ways. If there is a high volume of activities, then some form of self-assessment is optimal and relies on the activity owner determining the significance of their own activity. To steer this and improve the quality of the activity, a self-assessment questionnaire can be useful. These enshrine core architectural principles and measures of risk and can guide the assessor in their answers.

Recognize that there is an inherent weakness in any process that depends on self-assessments. There may be occurrences of optimism, whereby the self-assessor is not as an impartial as they should be, or instances of willful ignorance, where the self-assessor sets out to circumnavigate the processes in place. Either way, self-assessment is a tool that you will need to employ, so understanding and alleviating this predicament is key.

It helps to assume good intention and to *trust* the assessor while also introducing some form of quality assurance process to *verify* the accuracy of a sample of your respondents. This will help deter bad behavior, which may be "caught" during the quality assurance process. More importantly, it will help you identify any weaknesses in your process, especially where the same issues or misunderstandings arise repeatedly. If this assessment indeed deems an activity as significant, then a more detailed examination and review from an architecture team or review board may be required.

Architecture Review Board (ARB)

There are several definitions of the responsibilities of an architecture review board (ARB). In the context of the architecture review process, the ARB is accountable for providing a detailed assessment at each of the architecture tollgates and approving design and implementation activities. As such, it is important that the members of the ARB have relevant skills to assess the activity in question. Unsurprisingly, this aligns with the corresponding disciplines and levels of architecture.

You may require a number of ARBs, depending on the complexity, size, and scale of your organization. At Citigroup, there were over eight thousand applications and tens of thousands of development activities in a given year, with ARBs broadly aligning to the technology areas that supported different areas of the business: wholesale, retail, and corporate functions. In this way the ARB members had sufficient knowledge of the affected business, as well as comprehension of the portfolio of applications already in place. Each ARB then had the autonomy to assess their development activities.

There should, however, be consistency in how each ARB goes about doing this. This ensures that you're able to see the big picture as the CTO and to introduce a consistent set of consequences. The two outcomes of this process can be described succinctly as follows:

> **Conditions:** These are prerequisites that must be met to pass through the tollgate. Effectively, they block progress until such time as they can be shown to have been met.
>
> **Recommendations:** These are items that should be considered to guide the architecture activity but are not mandated and do not block progression through the tollgate.

As an example, a condition may be raised if additional analysis or design is needed to resolve some form of ambiguity or uncertainty. A recommendation may extoll the benefits of leveraging a particular technology product but does not mandate its usage.

Neither of these mechanisms should be used in the event of noncompliance with a policy or standard. Why not? There should be no discretion in complying with policies and standards, regardless of whether your activity is being assessed within an ARB or not. Yes, there may be occurrences of noncompliance, but these should refer back to your firm's policy exception process.

Architecture Review Process

The diagram that follows represents a pictorial representation of an architecture review process:

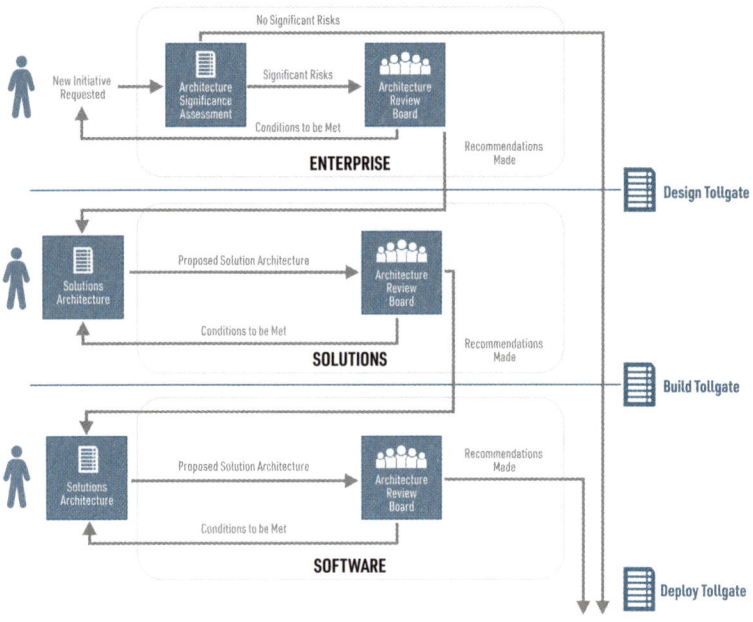

ARCHITECTURE REVIEW PROCESS FLOW

OPEN-SOURCE GOVERNANCE

Free and open-source software solutions are prevalent across most technology organizations, albeit the financial services industry has been slower to adopt them. This is due to the risk-averse nature of the industry as a whole, as well as innate beliefs that a company's proprietary software products have intrinsic value and contribute to their competitive advantage.

The reality is that, except for the most nuanced financial services solutions, such as algorithmic or automated trading products, there really isn't that much software that would truly generate a competitive advantage for a financial services company. The majority of the business capabilities that they require—HR solutions, client relationship management, and financial and regulatory reporting—are consistent with the requirements of many other industries.

Even if there is a financial services–specific solution, such as trade settlement, this does not necessarily generate competitive advantage, at least beyond the resilience and reliability of the solutions. In fact, harmonizing common products and solutions can simplify solving these types of problems. Collective adoption leads to dealing with bugs and issues and perfecting new features more rapidly. This is true of commercial software and free and open-source solutions; however, there are some specific risks associated with these solutions that merit specific governance oversight, especially if your firm wants to contribute to the development of the open-source software it uses, which I feel is imperative.

When considering the *consumption* of open-source technology products, they really should be treated much like any other commercially adopted solution. Your technology architecture governance should duly assess the merits and risks associated with the software product. Some aspects of third-party risk will differ from open source to commercial software, but the capability it provides and how it integrates into your portfolio of products should be consistent.

There are, however, significant differences when considering how your firm will *contribute* to open-source products. Contribution introduces a number of specific risks that you must understand and address: data leakage, reputational damage, noncompliance with the product's legal requirement, and the potential for loss of intellectual property. A dedicated committee can oversee these risks and ensure appropriate engagement. An industry term for this that is gaining prevalence is "Open Source Program Office."

Open Source Program Office (OSPO)

Establishing an Open Source Program Office creates an expert group that can establish the appropriate policies and standards to govern both the consumption and contribution to free and open-source projects. This group has the broad authority to address the following concerns and considerations:

Legal Compliance: There are several different license types and foundations under which open-source software can be published, each with varying expectations for the consumer regarding the use, modification, and distribution of the software. Permissive licenses such as the *Apache License*[35] and *MIT License*[36] expect the copyright notices to be included and propagated but indemnify the developer who modifies the code for their use to varying degrees. Copyleft licenses derive their name from the fact that the original software is copyrighted but with the requirement that, when it is distributed, it must provide rights to modify and use the code, including any software *derived* from the open source. This may not always be appropriate. There are many derivations from these two license types, with the Open Source Initiative[37] providing a resource to track them. Depending on the situation, vertical products may not be used because of their license conditions.

Data Leakage: If you are contributing code, or even documentation and comments, there is a risk that material information internal to your organization could be unwittingly, or even willfully, disclosed. Standards for contribution and often tooling for surveillance are required to address this. In addition, reputational damage could result if contributions do not meet your firm's communication standards.

Intellectual Property: Upon deciding to contribute to an existing open-source project or establishing a new one, consider the loss of intellectual property. You may ultimately need to establish external trademarks or patents before contribution. There may be the potential for revenue generation by the software, so assess the potential for that as well.

When contributing software, consider the type of contribution that you are making, as this can help establish the level of oversight required. The following provides some guidelines for different types of contributions, ranked from lowest to highest risk:

1. **Small Enhancement or Defect Fixes:** At this level the intent is only to ensure timely remediation of software defects or small enhancements. Historically, I have been at firms that "patched" defects onto their own internal copy of the software and believed this would expedite the process. However, this introduces significant complexity in tracking internal to external versions of the product and misses out on the benefits of collectively reviewing efficacy. Ensuring fixes and small enhancements are contributed to the core

public project simplifies the integration of the software and addresses these concerns. This level of engagement tends to be on an as-needed basis.

2. **Major Enhancements:** Where there is a need or desire to influence a software product, perhaps to better meet your firm's objectives, consider it a *major enhancement*. In these types of situations, a more proactive engagement with the project is required to help influence and steer the project. Project roles require time and effort to fully realize the associated benefits, so assess this early and up front.

3. **Project Contribution:** If you believe that you have created solutions that would benefit from being in the open-source domain, then you would be contributing as a moderator or "maintainer" of the project. This requires more than simply publishing and hoping for success. It often requires advocacy and real commitment to the project. Often, internally developed software is what ends up getting published as open source. In these situations I believe it is important for that team to "work in the open," applying their fixes and enhancements in the public domain. Too often, I have seen "shadow" efforts published externally while the internal product is more actively maintained—these types of efforts rarely realize their expected benefits.

Although not directly under the auspices of the OSPO, consideration should also be made on the treatment of *personal contributions* to open-source projects. As a technology organization, employees will join from other firms where they may have already contributed to a variety of projects. This, after all, is the nature of open-source contribution. Establish whether these contributions will continue to be permitted and how best to distinguish them from firm-sponsored contributions. As you consider all of this, the OSPO must inventory projects of interest, monitor and review contributions, and escalate any conflicts or nonobservance of standards as needed.

An OSPO ultimately has responsibility beyond governance and oversight. Within your firm, this should become an area of open-source competency and advocacy, one that encourages collaboration and contribution. A truism of open-source software is that, unlike proprietary internal projects, the contributors recognize that their contributions will be visible and likely assessed by their industry peers. This tends to result in high-quality contributions: more comprehensive documentation, broader test coverage, and ultimately, better code.

Inner Source

Some firms may decide to institute an *inner source* program, which, unlike open source, tries to apply an open-source culture of collaboration to proprietary internal projects. In my experience, they are rarely successful. This is mostly due to challenges around how the projects are funded and, more importantly, the limited impact and contributions that most firms, except for the largest technology firms, can muster. Rather than inner sourcing, you can realize significant benefits by looking to directly publish the target project into an open-source foundation, such as the Fintech Open Source Foundation, FINOS, mentioned earlier. This will enforce the same desirable rigor on the operation of the project while introducing potential benefits from contributions from other institutions.

EMERGING TECHNOLOGY GOVERNANCE

Much of the governance you establish will ensure appropriate use of various technology services and products, with much of this oversight being part of the governance of *applications* and *technology*. However, there is a nuance when considering emerging technology, whether that refers to technology products and solutions associated with *new* technologies or significant innovations to *existing* technologies. At the time of writing, the types of technology that may be considered as emerging include quantum computing—a new technology innovation—and large language models within artificial intelligence—an evolution of an existing technology.

Emerging technologies may offer significant advantages and opportunities, but they may also introduce new risks and challenges. As such, establish a framework to monitor and assess the technology landscape to determine if there are innovations of interest to your firm, and then consider the potential impact of adoption, both positive and negative.

Monitoring and Assessing the Technology Landscape

As a first step, monitor and assess the emerging technology landscape. This will take many forms. There are significant benefits to monitoring a number of disparate sources to ensure the completeness of your assessment. Media sources, such as *Bloomberg Businessweek* and *TechCrunch*, along with syndicated research materials from specialist firms such as Gartner, can help introduce new firms and technologies. Industry and open-source forums, such as Apache Software Foundation and the Linux Foundation, can provide insights into the focus for subject matter experts.

Regulators monitor emerging risks, which can also increase awareness of emerging technologies and their associated risks. Ultimately, your own technology staff will also provide their viewpoints. Finally, and this I would rely on the least, consulting firms will be happy to conduct research or share their perspectives with you . . . for a price.

The goal of this should be to shape an emerging technology report where you can categorize your interest, outline its relevance to your firm, and assess the maturity of the technology. You will probably not have the capacity to closely monitor everything, so at this stage, triage the most relevant and potentially beneficial technologies to a manageable list.

Assess the Consequences

Once a technology has matured to the degree that there is a real desire to leverage it within your firm, it is then necessary to more rigorously assess the real consequences of using the technology, both from the impact there may be to your business and, most importantly, the potential impact on your risks and controls. It may seem unusual to put such emphasis on the risks at this early stage. Regardless of how beneficial a technology product may be, if the risks associated with it outweigh the benefits, this must be understood earlier enough to steer investment accordingly. Discovering that the risks are too great after having invested significant time and money is, obviously, less than ideal.

At this stage, identifying subject matter experts—or perhaps more accurately, potential subject matter experts—is important. Establishing a working group or Delegated Action Group (covered in the chapter "'Just Enough' Oversight") to conduct this assessment, staffed with these experts, is a means to organically develop the necessary talent to incorporate the technology product.

Address the Gaps Necessary to Adopt

Once you understand the consequences of adopting the emerging technology, address any extant gaps in your policies, standards, procedures, governance oversight, or control implementations. At this stage it helps to establish controlled pilots to begin "proving out" the efficacy of the technology. Does it really deliver the expected benefits? Are the risks and controls appropriate for safe adoption in practice? As you mature in your understanding of the technology, iteratively improve how the technology is used, how you mitigate the risks, and how you implement the controls.

Early Production Usage

As you develop expertise across the workforce in an emerging technology, formally recognize this cohort of experts as a Center of Excellence to ensure continued focused research and oversight. This group will be ideally suited to manage external engagements if appropriate, whether in industry forums, working with regulators, or driving external investments or open-source engagement. They must ensure that as the technology develops, the governance and standards also develop and provide appropriate oversight. They will also drive early production usage for select requirements that help test the technology and its associated controls.

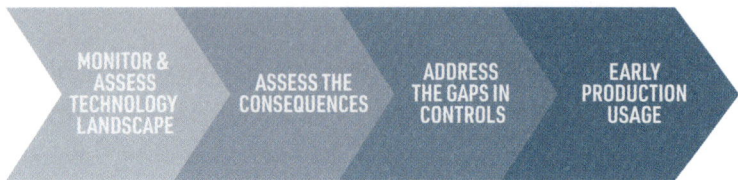

EMERGING TECHNOLOGY ASSESSMENT

When does *early production usage* become just being "business as usual?" For me, the litmus test that confirms whether a technology product has matured significantly enough to no longer warrant the emerging technology designation is (a) whether it is well understood by the broad technology population; (b) whether the policies, standards, and procedures are stable; and (c) whether the Center of Excellence is no longer necessary. At this stage, it may be beneficial to devolve that group into a *center of practice*. This group can help collate and propagate "best practices" for the use and adoption of the technology product but is no longer responsible for the oversight, which at this point should revert back to the core architecture governance forums.

STRATEGIC TECHNOLOGY INVESTMENT GOVERNANCE

As you develop appropriate strategies to support your firm's objectives, you need to secure the appropriate funding to support their delivery, perhaps extending over multiple years. It is very likely that your firm has some form of budgeting or capital management process in place, in which case your initiatives will be part of those processes. However, it is also beneficial to understand some of the considerations that will hopefully be in place when considering Strategic Technology Investments.

Fundamental to an effective oversight process is ensuring that for each investment, there is a correspondingly concise explanation of the objectives, drivers, and outcomes that support its funding. Strategic Technology Investment Governance, in the first instance, consists of reviewing these proposals to ensure the validity of the ask and the synergy—or lack thereof—with any outstanding investments that may be underway. Consider the proposed level of investment, time frames, risks, and constraints, and, if relevant, grant approval.

To make this judgment, it is critical to have an appropriately staffed investment review board. In addition to assessing the technology impact, they should understand the broader business, financial, and operational impact of the initiative in question. This is likely to be a senior executive group, led jointly by the chief financial officer (CFO) and technology head.

The firms I've worked with have usually met annually to approve new funding, with a half-year review of the progress of in-flight strategic investments. I feel that this is the absolute minimum and tend to advocate instead for quarterly reviews that evaluate the progress of existing investments and approve new projects as well.

Why? Anyone who has managed large technology programs understands a simple truth: what you plan to deliver and what you actually deliver are rarely the same. That is not to say objectives are *never* met, but over the course of a long project, significant technology challenges and opportunities inevitably present themselves. This may alter the *Strategic Investment Plan* considerably, something I introduce in the next section. Additional funding, new projects, or a reassessment of the validity of the existing initiatives may be necessary. After twelve months of investment, initiatives are rarely canceled—more often than not, the outcome and attitude at this stage is to double down and "get it over the line." By contrast, a more regular assessment that begins earlier in the project life cycle will help your team truly validate the assumptions made and determine the efficacy of your investments.

There are some challenges at this level in terms of investment "nimbleness," including predictable annual financial reporting. While I don't proclaim to be a CFO, my simplistic approach to this would be to create spending limits for strategic IT investments without a complete justification for the expense being in place. (The operational costs for running the technology estate, on the other hand, are far more predictable on an annual basis.) There would be a drawdown on this, with spending constrained to these agreed-upon annual limits. Here, I'll let my financial colleagues scoff at my proposal.

AI GOVERNANCE

Artificial intelligence (AI) has caught the public imagination more than any other technology innovation that I have recently seen, and I have been fortunate to have seen some pretty disruptive technologies arrive—and, in some instances, go. AI is here to stay, and it will have significant consequences across all industries and roles. At the very least, it will simplify and accelerate mundane and repetitive activities, augmenting and supporting human workers with quick, accurate, and personalized results. It may eventually even help eliminate certain activities or, at the very least, de-skill them to the point where previously specialized roles become more commoditized and thus cheaper, something termed Agentic AI. Let's face it: the machine doesn't eat, sleep, or take long vacations; will not make unforced errors; and will be unbiased in its judgment—at least within the parameters by which it has been trained.

What does all this mean from a technology perspective? AI certainly introduces complex ethical and regulatory challenges, but these challenges are not specific to the technology itself. They relate more to how and where AI is being used to solve specific *business* problems. From a pure technology standpoint, AI is just another technology product—an incredibly versatile and innovative solution but a technology product nevertheless.

At the risk of oversimplifying, from my perspective, AI provides a "black box" solution that's no different from procuring a commercial product from a third-party vendor to solve a specific problem. We do not know the intricacies of how the product works, nor the details on how it was built; we simply judge the product on whether it delivers the expected outcomes that drove us to purchase it and whether it complies with our firm's technology and security standards. So from a *technology* governance perspective, it should fit into the existing oversight by which all other technology solutions are governed.

What about when technologists use AI to support the development of applications that affect their business processes? Surely, this introduces additional complexity—I can almost hear you shout. Yet in my humble opinion, this is not so. Yes, previously complex and skilled programming and development activities will be augmented through the use of AI products. Microsoft, for example, provides a generative AI Copilot development stack, a comprehensive set of tools that can create code, analyze existing code, refactor solutions, and generally improve the overall quality of the code—and the productivity of the engineer. It is truly amazing stuff. But until the machine does all this unsupervised and can account for ensuring the appropriateness of the code and its compliance with technology and cybersecurity standards, the core responsibility remains with the human engineer. If anything, the risk profile may, in fact, be reduced, as an "augmented" developer benefits from being paired with an AI expert who follows rules unwaveringly.

From a technology perspective, I see minimal impact here. But to reiterate, the use of AI will require a very careful assessment at any firm. It currently lacks the explainability of existing coded solutions, so understanding *why* it makes certain determinations remains opaque, although this is an area of significant innovation.

It will obviously lack emotional intelligence and common sense—at least at the time of writing—so it will be unable to adapt and recognize emotional cues. It is also expensive, in terms of both time and resources, so its inclusion truly needs to merit the level of investment required. I would posit that if you can solve a problem with traditional approaches, continue to do so.

One of the harder aspects to quantify in the realm of AI relates to these ethical challenges. Ethics are imprecise and influenced by an individual's upbringing, culture, and even religion. As such, ensuring that AI systems operate within ethical boundaries will require robust governance frameworks and clear ethical guidelines. Even then, what is ethical for one group may not be for another.

CHAPTER 9

"JUST ENOUGH" OVERSIGHT

When individual members of the team are highly disciplined, they can be trusted and, therefore, allowed to operate with very little oversight.

—JOCKO WILLINK

At every organization that I have ever worked at, there have been a number of different mechanisms by which design and development decisions are made. Design forums, working groups, councils, committees, team meetings, advisory bodies, and project forums, all with the express intent of "making decisions" or "providing oversight." As well-intentioned as these groups were at initiation, they invariably lost their way. Why? Usually it was because the original intent was lost, or the original members lost interest and delegated responsibilities to others who felt compelled to revisit decisions that prior incumbents had felt resolved. Rarely, if ever, would the group decide that they had finally finished.

As the CTO of an organization with over forty-five thousand

engineers, I quickly realized that I needed to develop an approach to address these shortcomings. I needed to appropriately surveil the design and development activities underway while ensuring that the procedures I introduced would not be cumbersome or difficult to follow. I needed to subsume all prior approaches to "design forums" or "working groups" and generate a number of key outcomes, including the following:

- *Why are we doing this?*
- *Why is it important?*
- *What are we trying to achieve?*
- *Who is accountable? Who should be informed?*
- *How do we measure progress?*
- *How will we decide when we are finished?*

The framework I established laid out simple steps that could be applied to resolve many different types of challenges, whether developing new operational procedures, creating policies and standards, or engaging in low-level design activities. I called my framework *Delegated Action Groups* (DAGs)—regardless of the problem being addressed, a group was being assembled and given the authority to look into resolving a specific problem.

DELEGATED ACTION GROUPS

A Delegated Action Group, or DAG as they became known, is simply a group assembled by a sponsoring organization and given sufficient authority to resolve a specific concern. A number of core concepts should be considered in their formation.

The POCS Statement: Problem, Outcomes, Constraints, and Skills

Successful oversight must succinctly define not only the *Problem* that needs to be addressed but also precisely why it is critical to complete at this time. Any imprecision or ambiguity in this regard severely impedes the likelihood of success. If you don't know what you are looking to address, then you have very little chance of addressing it—and even if you did, how would you recognize it once you had done so?

A key aspect in defining the problem statement is ensuring that all participants agree on and understand the intent. This means that the sponsors—the individual or group who identified the problem that needs addressing—must initially articulate the problem statement in the language they understand. They must detail why the problem needs to be addressed and what they believe needs to be achieved. The sponsors should also consider any *Constraints*, including critical business, technical, or time constraints that may shape the resolution.

Finally, they must consider the primary *Skills* required by the participants to whom they intend to delegate the authority to address the problem, including technical, business, or legal skills. They should then identify the individual with the appropriate skills whom they intend to lead the group to resolution.

This individual's first responsibility is to review and, if needed, challenge the problem statement. Any and all ambiguity and vagueness must be resolved, whether in the problem statement itself, the constraints that have been identified, or the participants' necessary skills. The lead must be confident that they fully comprehend *what* is needed and *why* they are the most appropriate person to lead. They can then work with the sponsors to assemble an appropriate group to finally address the problem.

At the initial meeting with the broader group, it is again necessary to review the problem statement, the constraints, and the ultimate goal. All participants should understand this and know why they are relevant to the group. Once they are in agreement, which may require iterations with the sponsors, their first action is to distill this statement to one or more *Outcomes* that they feel will effectively and completely address the problem.

So as not to become unbounded, the framework presents a number of predetermined types of outcomes—a specification, a plan, a budget—that ensure some level of consistency. Normally more than one outcome would be needed. Once this statement has been fully finalized, then the group can proceed with meeting and delivering the agreed-upon outcomes.

Structuring the Delegated Action Group

Now that the group has been assembled, how exactly should it operate? For me, this is a key aspect of the oversight framework. Here, I will not mandate how they operate, including their frequency, participation of core members, the memorialization of minutes, and so forth. None of that is ultimately important, and moreover, dictating that level of operation creates overhead and bureaucracy. The lead and their assembled group can decide all these things themselves according to their view on what will be required to address the specifics of their POCS statement. So then how do I, as the CTO, surveil and ensure appropriate oversight if there is zero conformity from group to group?

Decision Records (DRs)

For delegation and oversight to be effective, the efficacy of the DAG must be assessed. A traditional approach may involve embedding independent assessors, reviewing meeting minutes and artifacts, or having each group provide some form of conformed status report. Given the subjective nature of these types of assessments, none of these approaches necessarily scale or provide high confidence in terms of a specific group's effectiveness. In my experience, they also tend to focus on reporting or assessing *what is happening* instead of the *decisions* and *progress* being made.

This oversight framework mandates an alternative mechanism for tracking the effectiveness of a DAG: the *Decision Record*, or DR. This conformed entry memorializes each *significant* decision that the group has made as they proceed toward delivering a specific outcome. To be explicit, the minutiae on *how* the decision was made is not of relevance. We only want *what* the actual decision *is* and the specific consequence of that decision. This is a nice way of ensuring that the decision in question is indeed "significant"—if there is no consequence, it probably isn't.

This is an incredibly powerful surveillance mechanism, as an absence of decisions signifies that progress is not being made. At this point the sponsor can intervene to determine the root cause. Perhaps there is still ambiguity in the problem statement or outcomes. Perhaps the participants do not have the necessary skills. Or perhaps they are not meeting at all.

Of course, assuming decisions *are* being recorded, the sponsors can review the details. Do they seem appropriate as significant decisions? Is the lineage to how they will help resolve an outcome apparent? Are they being made in a timely manner? This transparency allows appropriate surveillance and intervention when necessary.

Finally, there is another powerful benefit in recording significant decisions and outcomes: they provide an *explanation* to future observers, either after the DAG has completed or for additional members who join the DAG after its initiation. Now there is a mechanism through which they can understand the rationale behind the decisions without necessarily forcing the whole group to reset and explain. Newcomers may not agree with the decisions, but at least the supporting context and rationale are available to them.

Verification and Review

This lightweight structure ensures enough consistent data across the various DAGs to allow the CTO to complete a number of other verifications and reviews:

- *Are multiple active DAGs looking at the same or similar problems?* Here, there is an opportunity to consolidate or combine different DAGs, cancel one or more of them, or consciously make the decision to allow many to execute and make a determination of the best outcomes upon conclusion.

- *Are new DAGs being proposed for which a previous completed DAG exists?* A common occurrence in my experience is that if a team is unhappy with a previous outcome, they can quietly revisit and recast those decisions. By having to create a DAG, these situations surface and can be addressed.

- *Were outcomes introduced for which there is no lineage to a DAG?* The framework is not particularly onerous or bureaucratic, so willfully avoiding creating a DAG should not occur. However, when it does—and it will—a retrospective DAG can be initiated to memorialize the decisions and outcomes. That is a burden for the team but one that they instigated in the first place, so have little sympathy.

Where to Memorialize DAGs, POCS, and DRs

For this oversight to be successful, you need to systemize it in a way that makes it easy to find, initiate, and execute DAGs. In my experience, any simple workflow system that allows configuration of data to be captured will suffice. I have had good success with *Atlassian Jira*[38] in creating templates for the (a) Problem, Constraints, and Skills statement; (b) Outcomes, as there may be multiple required to address the Problem; and (c) DRs—again, there will likely be multiples of these to support the Outcomes.

However, although Jira provides a number of significant benefits and is already well understood by many technologists, it is not terribly user-friendly for some senior stakeholders. For that reason I have always created a simple management dashboard that summarizes the key fields in an easy-to-consume manner, and this has then been made available to the whole firm. The more transparency and exposure that the DAGs have, the less likely comments such as "I had no idea you had looked at that!" will become. There is a facility for everyone to review ongoing and completed DAGs. My experience has shown that when folks know that their work will be viewed by a broad—and senior—population, pride and diligence follow.

WHERE A DELEGATED ACTION GROUP MAY HELP

Anytime there is a need to gain consensus for complex or contentious problems, a DAG will provide the structure, transparency, and rigor required. The following are some of the areas where a DAG has helped me significantly:

Determine Approach for AI Governance: AI is a transformative technology that, especially in years past, has not been well understood. A useful initial Outcome within this DAG was simply creating an agreed-upon definition of AI. After all, it's pretty difficult to govern something that you do not understand or cannot define. Although AI is broadly understood as a machine mimicking human intelligence and problem-solving, it actually lacks a precise industry definition. Many solutions can appear "intelligent" but are based on traditional technologies and approaches. Many assume that AI means some level of autonomous decision-making—"Skynet," here we come! Statistical modeling is an important aspect of AI, but should it be considered AI? In any case there is yet plenty of contention and thus a need for transparency and rigor. Once we agreed on a definition, it was significantly easier to assess existing governance forums and approaches to determine if any were suitable, which our existing model governance processes were ultimately deemed to be.

Determine the Developer Experience Strategy: What does *good* look like for a developer? How do we integrate the right controls while creating an innovating and rewarding environment that improves productivity and enthusiasm? This is a broad topic that drew many opinions and benefited from bringing together a variety of subject matter experts, each with different experiences and priorities—perfect for a DAG.

Determine Approach to Open-Source Contributions: This is more of a challenge in financial services than some other industries, but clearly outlining the rationale for why this was important and beneficial to the firm required rigor and discussion at every level. We had to go beyond technologists—this DAG had to include contributions from risk, compliance, and legal teams.

Evaluate <Product> to Provide <Capability>: There will always be a multitude of products that profess to fulfill a required capability. A DAG can ensure that the criteria for success are rigorously applied and identify any constraints that must be considered when selecting a new technology or security product, whether it is technical, security-related, or financial. Transparency and collaboration help choose the right product for clear reasons. This is extremely useful when you need to provide a rationale when the next supersmart technologist who joins your firm is aghast at the product you chose.

Hopefully these admittedly simple examples show why and where leveraging a DAG makes sense. These were not "coffee morning" meetings. Each had to include different people to be successful; convene with a clear, unambiguous objective; be easily monitored and surveilled; and make real decisions that resulted in new policies, standards, and strategies.

PART III
STRATEGY

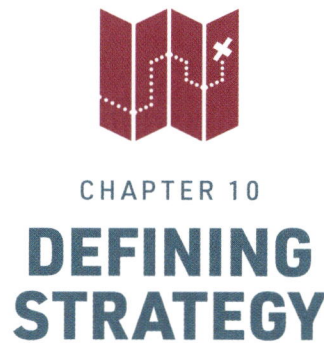

CHAPTER 10

DEFINING STRATEGY

A vision without a strategy remains an illusion.
—LEE BOLMAN

When considering how best to define your strategies, it is important to understand the connection to your firm's overall *vision* statement. What is a vision statement? It is broadly accepted to be the forward-looking statement that defines where your company aspires to be. It should be aspirational and ambitious, succinct and unambiguous, usually a single sentence or two. Its purpose is to focus the whole firm on driving together toward the realization of a common vision.

As such, all areas—business, technology, and operations—should consider how their strategies support and connect to the vision. Without pertinent strategies to support it, the vision will be vaporous and meaningless. Likewise, without a concise vision statement, how will you assess the efficacy and appropriateness of the subordinate strategies, and how will the different areas of the firm ensure connectivity and cohesion? One requires the other.

As your firm's CTO, you will be expected to conceive and communicate your *technology* strategies and areas of focus that support the realization of the broader vision. You will likely need many disparate strategies that cover a number of key technology topics: developer productivity, infrastructure rationalization, adoption of emerging technology, and so on. Your technology objectives will likely be key *enablers* of the strategies from other areas of your firm, so you will also need to link your strategies to these other areas.

To achieve this, first, consider how best to structure your thoughts. At the most basic level, your strategies must answer the following core questions:

- What are we trying to achieve?
- What challenges or constraints must we consider?
- What will be required for this to be successful?
- How will we track progress through to completion?

This may seem obvious, but in my experience, I have seen many instances where a high-level vision statement alone is touted as the strategy. But a single "big picture" statement of intent lacks the details a true strategy would require. Likewise, I have also seen many strategy documents that focus on microscopically detailed *activities* that should be undertaken, without being concise about the actual *objectives* and *success criteria* that are the focus of the activities. It may have merit, but it is probably too detailed to be an overarching strategy. So then how do we best determine our strategies?

STRENGTHS, WEAKNESSES, OPPORTUNITIES, AND THREATS

A Strengths, Weaknesses, Opportunities, and Threats (SWOT)[39] analysis is a well-established technique to evaluate a set of actions. In my experience, these provide a balanced perspective on internal and external factors that may influence your decisions. Strengths and Weaknesses refer to *internal* factors, whereas the Opportunities and Threats refer to *external* factors. When considering areas of focus for your technology strategies—or assessing the efficacy of existing strategies—this simple assessment framework can be a useful tool.

A SWOT analysis can help guide broad macro strategies by asking open-ended questions such as, *What do we do well? What could we do better?* And *Where do we face external jeopardy or competition?* While this approach is valid, I have found it far more useful when applied to a known objective or outcome because it helps shape and guide the assessment and highlights your strategic imperatives.

For example, perhaps your firm has an existing storage strategy predicated on the use of a relational database product hosted internally in your data center. This may not necessarily be a strategy; more likely it's just "always been that way." In this instance, a SWOT analysis can help you evaluate the merits of the existing approach and determine whether there might be a benefit to amending or creating a new technology strategy.

The *Strengths* you may identify for this hypothetical example include the following:

- The internal workforce understands the existing products, development approach, and tooling currently in use. This is definitely a positive, as any change will mean retraining staff and perhaps amending development practices.

- Existing applications have already been engineered to use the current products. (Let's say 70 percent of the current *applications* make use of the relational database products.) So there is already critical mass in place. A change would necessitate significant rework and associated operational risk.

The *Weaknesses* could include the following:

- The existing storage solutions are expensive to maintain, including the cost of hygiene and patching activities that take place internally to maintain them. Anything hosted in our data center needs patching to ensure an acceptable security posture and optimal performance.

- Existing solutions are expensive to scale for expanding data requirements. Granted, this would depend on the actual product in use, but this is a hypothetical example.

- An expensive internal workforce with niche expertise is required to engineer and maintain the products.

- New techniques that are in demand by your development community are not currently supported. (This is unfortunately nearly always true. Developers have a knack for identifying the latest and greatest at an amazing velocity.)

The *Opportunities* may include the following:

- Existing vendors may be keen to partner on the development of new features.

- Existing vendors may be open to negotiating favorable commercial terms to continue using their products.

The *Threats* may include the following:

- The existing vendors may *not* be open to negotiating favorable commercial terms to continue using their product but rather, given the "lock-in" (remember 70 percent of the existing applications are using the products), may drive their pricing up.
- External expertise in the product is a diminishing pool. (This would very much depend on the product, but at large enterprises where many solutions may be decades old, this is a real threat.)

No doubt, in reality, there would be many more items in this list. The value of this exercise is driving and shaping your analysis. Often, there is a corollary between two items, such as the opportunity to negotiate favorable terms versus the threat that your existing vendor will amend terms less favorably. Further investigation will be required to determine which will ultimately manifest.

At the most basic level, once you determine the details behind these statements, you can assess the merits of the overall approach. *Do the Strengths outweigh the Weaknesses? Do the Opportunities outweigh the Threats?* Associate a relative importance weighting with each statement, as not all will be of equal importance. Your weightings may be subjective—as are the statements themselves—but at the very least, they should help provide a later explanation for why you developed your strategy.

STRATEGIC INVESTMENT PLANS

Once you have determined the focus of your strategies, you need a sustainable mechanism to define, govern, and report on progress toward your intended strategic objectives. It must do the following things:

- Operate consistently across all initiatives, including those originated directly to support specific strategies, as well as those that indirectly contribute to the strategies in other parts of your firm.

- Demonstrate that your sustained strategic investments are indeed realizing their intended objectives.

- Be easy to consume and facilitate comparisons across different strategies. Which are successful? Which are cost-effective? Which should be refined, rewritten, or rescinded?

To address these challenges, I developed a simple methodology to define strategic plans to which many initiatives could be contributors: *Strategic Investment Plans*. It provides a mechanism to concisely describe a set of objectives that represent your strategic intent. It provides details on the outcomes that must be delivered to meet the objectives. It also allows varied initiatives to be mapped to the same strategy and includes specifics on how their deliverables or milestones will contribute to the completion of the strategy. Finally, it should also provide a mechanism to demonstrate and report on the efficacy and outcomes being delivered and ultimately demonstrate both the impact and sustainability of your strategies.

Let's consider another contrived but fairly prevalent example:

a Strategic Investment Plan to support *Public Cloud Adoption*. We can assume that we have completed the necessary SWOT analysis and confirmed that it indeed makes sense to embark on a given strategy. This is a far-reaching program, so we can be sure that there will be a need for many different initiatives for it to be successful. However, we must ensure that *how* exactly each initiative will contribute to overall success is both well understood and agreed upon. It will also be important to consider existing initiatives or projects already in progress, which may also contribute to the overall strategy.

The fundamental components of a Strategic Investment Plan include the core objectives that motivate and drive the strategy, the outcomes that should be evidence that the objectives are being met, and specific trackable *milestones* that will ensure the successful delivery of the outcomes.

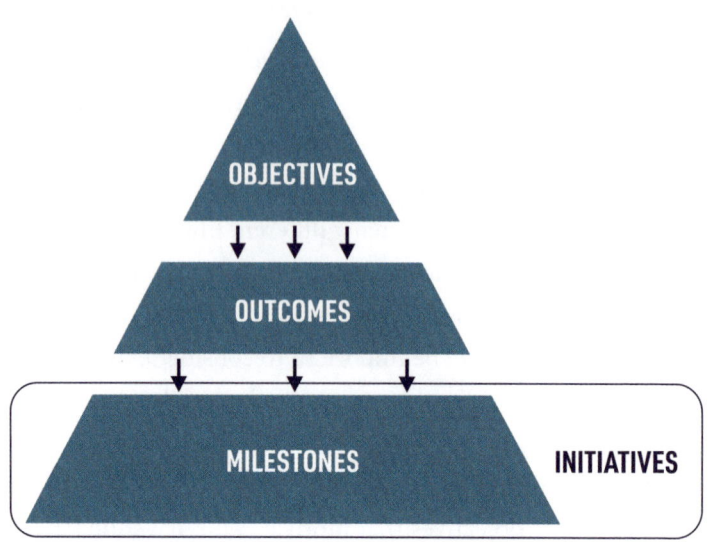

FUNDAMENTAL COMPONENTS OF A STRATEGIC INVESTMENT PLAN

There are several *sections* that should captured to support these components, and now I'll provide some context on why each section is needed, how it contributes to the overall strategy, and some things to take into account when writing each section.

1. Background

This first section provides a high-level, stakeholder-friendly description of the motivations and drivers that are underpinning the creation of the strategy. Much of this may be provided from the SWOT analysis. It should contextualize the opportunity, problem, or risk that is looking to be addressed, along with the anticipated benefits. This high-level summary of the problem statement encourages comprehension and support for your strategy. If senior stakeholders fundamentally disagree with your description, addressing and resolving the issue early is of paramount importance. The primary consideration when writing this section is to use plain language, without industry jargon or acronyms, so that it can be easily understood, without additional embellishment or narrative being required.

For our Public Cloud Adoption example, we would most likely detail the potential economic and resilience benefits that could be realized by leveraging services provided by the Public Cloud provider, as well as the potential for higher degrees of automated hygiene and controls. Of course, this would heavily depend on appropriate application architectures to realize these benefits. Moving existing applications to the cloud without re-architecture—sometimes termed as "lift and shift"—would very likely introduce considerably more operational risk and increased costs.

2. Objectives

This key section requires appropriate detail on the strategy's overall success criteria. What must be achieved, and how will successful execution be measured? It should provide details on the strategic objectives, the specific drivers behind each objective, and the macro measures or indicators that will be used to evidence success.

When writing this section, consider creating meaningful categories to group related objectives, including the business impact, the technical constraints, or indeed, the regulatory requirements. The same or related measures may then be appropriate to evidence the success criteria for more than one similarly categorized objective.

For our Public Cloud Adoption example, key objectives would include the ability to develop and deploy applications on the public cloud service provider (CSP). Additionally, there should be tangible and measurable objectives, perhaps ones related to the desired commercial outcomes or to scale and elasticity—such as the ability for an application to seamlessly accommodate peak demands with no manual intervention. From a resilience perspective, perhaps it should demonstrate the ability to deploy and automatically leverage different regions and availability zones or, better yet, the ability to deploy applications on more than one CSP. Albeit migration between CSP would involve reengineering, a multicloud approach ensures flexibility in choosing which services to leverage with which CSP and helps avoid "lock-in" with one specific provider.

3. Outcomes

This section simply lists the key outcomes that will collectively satisfy the strategy's stated objectives. These may represent the introduction of something new—systems, processes, or products—or the elimination of something, such as a manual process, a legacy product, or an inadequate system.

Each outcome must be demonstrably complete. For example, it may not be sufficient that a new system is in production; rather, evidence of its successful adoption may be a more meaningful outcome, such as the number of clients leveraging the application.

This is an important section—the overall success and comprehension of the strategy may well depend on how well crafted it is. Include descriptions of the relevant outcomes and categories. Indicate which objectives the outcome supports. Include a measure of success that is specific, measurable, achievable, realistic, and time-bound (*SMART*[40]). And ensure that outcomes are uniquely identified, as specific milestones from later initiatives will need to be mapped to them.

Looking at our Public Cloud Adoption example again, the following may be pertinent outcomes, again not exhaustive but, at the very least, representative:

- Establish an appropriate security program, including a security operations center, to ensure automated monitoring for all applications and services running on a specific CSP, with vulnerability and incident response being fully integrated into existing procedures. A measure of success could be a successful evaluation of controls and monitoring by a "Red Team," or ethical hacking group.

- Establish appropriately configured infrastructure services needed to host applications, including identity and access management, network, monitoring, logging, and inventory. A measure of success would be the availability of such services on a specific CSP.

- Establish appropriately configured application foundational services needed to build and deploy applications, including compute, storage, and the software development life cycle services. A measure of success would be the availability of such services on a specific CSP.

- Establish the first business application and associated services, engineered to benefit from the intrinsic advantages of executing on a CSP and fully leveraging all security, infrastructure, and application foundational services. A measure of success could be its availability and adoption in production.

- Establish all of these elements on more than one CSP.

4. Enterprise Architecture Mapping

We've already discussed different aspects of architecture and the kinds of artifacts and approaches that are appropriate for different disciplines. The alignment of the strategic plan to the Enterprise Architecture Level—particularly the Business discipline outputs—is key. This ensures that everything pertinent is anchored to a specific set of Business Architecture objectives.

As with all artifacts, the strategic plan should, at the very least, be mapped to the relevant Business Architecture taxonomies, ensuring that investment spend and benefits themselves are mapped and tracked. As you reap the benefits of your plan, it should be reflected in relevant Business Architecture progress metrics. If your strategy pertains to data programs, linkage to Information Architecture outputs, such as the in-scope data concepts and associated Logical Data Models, also makes sense.

Looking at previously listed outcomes for the Public Cloud Adoption example, only the outcome that relates to a specific business application would be appropriate to map to the relevant business process, functions, or data concept taxonomy. However, the other services would map to either Technology or Security Architecture taxonomies.

5. Proposed Logical Architecture

This optional section is very much dependent on the strategy being described. Often, for clarity of communication, some form of simplified architectural view can provide a concise description of the proposed solution that the accompanying strategy aims to introduce. This pictorial representation is not as detailed as the Solutions Architecture artifacts described earlier, but it does provide a mechanism for the specific initiatives associated with the strategy to map back to. It also provides specifics in terms of how they help realize the strategy.

As initiatives are completed, more of the Logical Architecture will be implemented. Often, as initiatives are completed, what is learned in the process leads to revisions, which are both acceptable and to be expected.

The diagram that follows provides a sample of the elements that could be used to create a Logical Architecture wiring diagram. It's by no means sacrosanct; it merely provides a comprehensive example of the types of components and data flows that should be considered. That said, it is both comprehensive and simple enough to cater for most solutions at a high level of fidelity.

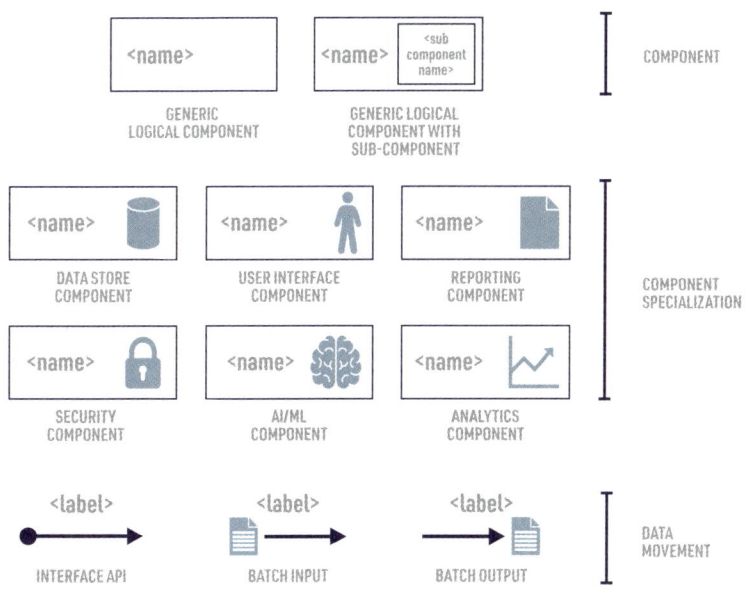

EXAMPLE LEGEND FOR LOGICAL ARCHITECTURE DIAGRAMS

If we consider the Public Cloud Adoption example, there is a simplified diagram that could be helpful in terms of orienting initiatives to where they are contributing. I have not detailed the specifics of the Business Application, but this representation of what may be included should suffice:

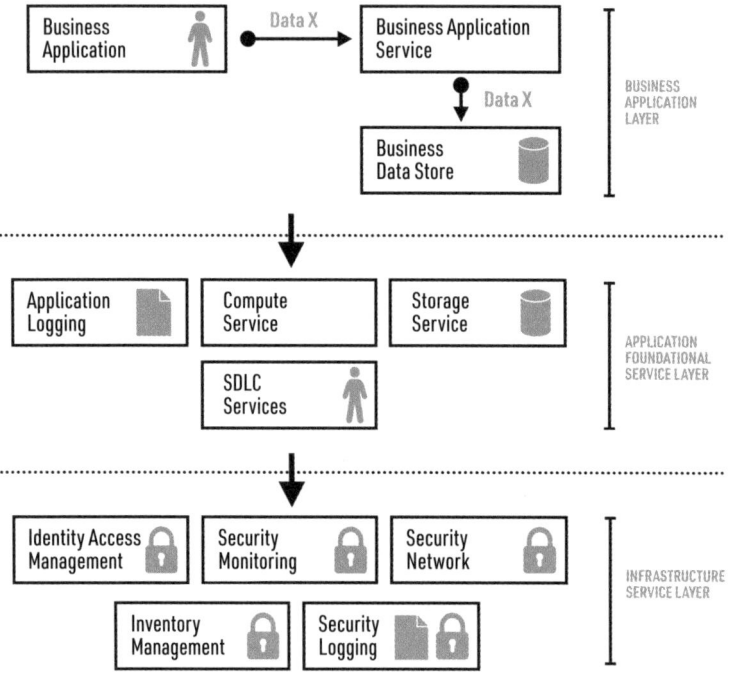

HIGH-LEVEL LOGICAL ARCHITECTURE FOR PUBLIC CLOUD ADOPTION EXAMPLE

Again, this simplified diagram is not meant to be a comprehensive design artifact. What it does provide is a navigation aid to where associated initiatives will contribute. Were this a real strategy, there would almost certainly be a set of initiatives to deliver Infrastructure Services, Application Foundations, and the Business Application itself. Each of these initiatives would likely consist of a number of specific programs and projects undertaken to meet the overall outcomes.

6. Mapping to New and Existing Initiatives

There may be existing *legacy* initiatives underway that may not be associated with a current strategy. Initiatives may have originated as a result of other historic business drivers, or they may be long-lived initiatives or ones that have evolved significantly since their inception, where the rationale behind them is less well understood than it once was. For these, it is equally important to be able to memorialize the impact or consequence of continued investment, especially where they may have an indirect or direct impact on current strategies.

Ultimately, you execute your strategy through one or more relevant initiatives in support of specific outcomes that further your firm's strategic objectives. Assess *all* initiatives—both those already in progress and those that are newly proposed. This may seem arduous, but given that (a) all existing initiatives should have an association with the Business, Technology, or Security taxonomies, and (b) the Strategic Investment Plan also has an association with the same taxonomies, identifying the subset of relevant existing initiatives is comparatively straightforward.

Once they've been identified, assess the initiatives to see if they support specific objectives and outcomes. Next, assess the completeness and coverage necessary to accomplish the strategy. If specific outcomes are not yet addressed, then create additional initiatives as needed. It is very likely that any significant strategy will require multiyear investments to complete, so having unmapped objectives at the onset is not all uncommon. There may be critical dependencies to be completed to meet your objectives.

In our Public Cloud Adoption example, it would not be possible to execute the programs and projects to build the business application without the infrastructure and application foundational services first being in place—the kind of effort that could easily take more than a year.

The cost of existing initiatives should be well understood. For missing initiatives meant to complete unaddressed outcomes, even those that are deferred because of other dependencies, it is important to at least determine some high-level perspective of their likely costs. Why? This allows you to assess your strategy's total cost, which is naturally important when assessing cost-benefit. Do the likely benefits outweigh the probable costs? Obviously, this only relates to indicative costs. Without detailed analysis, you run the risk of higher actual costs—in my experience they rarely diminish.

When associating new and existing initiatives, recognize that your strategy may be valid for a number of years, so it's important to note key initiative stakeholders, including sponsors, program and project leads, and technical architects. Over time these may change, but understanding who is actually responsible for the delivery of the initiatives is important, as you may call upon them for progress reports.

7. Key Milestones

Especially when mapping existing initiatives to a new strategy, there is a high likelihood that not everything related to the associated projects contributes directly to the strategy. Perhaps a different strategy resulted in the creation of the initiative, with an ancillary benefit to other later strategies. As such, it is important to explicitly identify the specific project milestones that are supporting the strategy and to disambiguate them from the other irrelevant activities.

This section should provide those details, identifying the

specific milestones that should be tracked as part of this strategy. For traceability, record details on the deliverable and key dates. This ensures that you only need to report the relevant details from the associated project, which is important to ensure precision and relevance in any updates provided.

With our Public Cloud Adoption example, it would be easy to conceive of existing projects that have some relevance to your strategy that also need mapping. For instance, imagine there is an existing identity and access management strategy (IAMS) that examines all aspects of IAMS, private and public cloud. It would provide the requisite infrastructure for this strategy, though only the milestones specifically related to the public cloud would be mapped here.

8. Risks and Issues

It is important to track any specific risks that may affect your strategy. A risk is a potential obstacle that may arise in the future but just as likely may not. While your initial SWOT analysis may have identified macro weaknesses and threats that *could* become risks to your strategy, it is more likely that you will need to identify new risks. Of course, you can also escalate any existing risks and issues in the associated initiatives, programs, or projects and include them here.

When recording a risk or issue, identify an accountable owner who can assess the materiality of the risk or issue and the potential impact to the strategy that it presents. If there is a high likelihood of a risk occurring, note the mitigation required. If it is an existing issue that has already materialized with negative consequences to your strategy, detail the actions being taken to resolve it, including time frames.

TRACKING PROGRESS

As any strategy progresses, you must determine whether you're making progress toward realizing your strategic objectives. It is just as important to understand if there are risks, issues, or other concerns to address. Many will be associated with their related initiatives, programs, and projects. As such, track them according to your firm's program and project management standards and procedures, which will be wholly dependent on the methodologies and tools being used. Though I won't cover those details here, I will emphasize the importance of effectively tracking the life cycle of your strategies, which entails a set of specific considerations at their *Origination*, *Execution*, and *Closure*.

Origination

Once you've determined that a new strategy is required, create a proposed Strategic Investment Plan and complete each relevant section. Once you have, you can review this comprehensive plan with key stakeholders. There are a few important considerations at this stage. An obvious place to start is to weigh the merits and benefits of the proposed strategy against the levels of investment required and the associated risks. Another key consideration is whether there are existing strategies in play that overlap or collide with your new strategy.

Our Business, Technology, and Security taxonomies will help here; once they're associated with your existing strategies, they should provide a simple filter to identify *potentially related* strategies. It may be that amending an existing strategy is preferable to introducing a new one, avoiding confusion and ambiguity and most probably accelerating realization of outcomes.

Execution

Once approved and in execution, periodically review your progress in achieving your strategic objectives. Mapped initiatives will already be monitored according to your program and project management oversight, but be sure to consolidate the risks, issues, and changes that relate to the Strategic Investment Plan. Assess the impact and make adjustments accordingly. Periodic reviews also introduce a cadence through which you can update all interested parties. As with all things, transparency is important.

A more invasive review should take place in line with your firm's investment planning cycle, which at most should be an annual activity. This provides an opportunity to introduce new initiatives as critical dependencies are completed and to amend existing initiatives. In all cases incremental funding will be required, so it is important to ensure your benefits case is still valid. At this cadence it is also important to refresh the core content of your Strategic Investment Plan to ensure that all sections remain accurate and complete. If you decide, upon review, to abandon a strategy early—which I would consider a successful outcome—ensure that strategies only proceed if the corresponding benefits are being realized and strong stakeholder support remains.

Closure

Your Strategic Investment Plan has reached its conclusion with its core objectives having been satisfactorily met. While this might seem simple, agreeing on closure can become contentious when there are outstanding activities or items required to ensure the strategy's continued success. This is where the success criteria you defined at inception, and potentially modified during execution, become even more important. If these have indeed been met satisfactorily, then closure is appropriate, and your strategy should no longer be subject to ongoing monitoring and reporting. Meanwhile, related deliverables—applications, processes, and services—can continue to be monitored and developed as part of the normal investment, program and project management oversight.

LONG-FORM THINKING

In the course of my career, I have seen the attention span and appetite to read and digest information diminish notably in all aspects of society, and this observation is supported by a number of US Bureau of Labor Statistics surveys. (For example, from 2003 to 2018, the average amount of time Americans spent reading for personal interest per day fell by six minutes, to less than sixteen minutes per day.[41])

Unfortunately, this has also been true in the corporate world, including at most of the firms with which I have worked. More and more, there has been a drive to condense, summarize, and abridge information to make it quicker and easier to consume. As a consequence, details that are crucial for true comprehension are often obfuscated or wholly removed. When it comes to conceiving and introducing multiyear strategies with potentially large sums of investment dollars and significant deliverables, this has always felt to me a wholly erroneous approach and a "false economy."

I have developed a reputation for being "the White Paper Guy," a moniker I am proud to have earned. I firmly believe in the importance of digging into the details when ordering and organizing your thoughts and presenting ideas with confidence. Ideas easily represented in a single bullet in a presentation suddenly seem a lot more onerous when supporting details are required.

I am not alone in seeing things this way. Jeff Bezos famously wrote in an investor letter, "We don't do PowerPoint (or any other slide-oriented) presentations at Amazon. Instead, we write narratively structured six-page memos. We silently read one at the beginning of each meeting in a kind of study hall."[42] This six-page format forces conciseness and clarity but is also sufficiently long-form that it necessitates a level of detail to explain and support both discussion and potential challenges. I would strongly endorse that you embrace this approach, especially as you formulate your strategies. While it is extremely simple to summarize details if required from a long-form document, going from a summary to the details is nowhere near as easy.

CHAPTER 11

THE TARGET OPERATING MODEL

It takes a pair of fresh eyes to see, but more importantly to perceive, what's missing in an organization.

—PEARL ZHU

As the CTO, you will ideally be responsible for both technology engineering and operational activities. It will be necessary for you to assess the efficacy of any existing organizations that you inherit and to design an appropriate operating model to support the execution and implementation of your strategies. Your operating model must be able to create a sustainable and defensible organization and respond to changes in business objectives—and the associated strategy—in a clear and structured way. This will support the creation of established, targeted hiring plans, which themselves will ensure that there are appropriate accountabilities and ownership across your organization.

As with many of the items in this book, I strongly endorse that the operating model you design represent a *target state*. Again, it is important to design your target organization without any of the existing constraints so as to create an idealized operating model. This will make it possible to evaluate the gaps between the current organization and the target one and amend hiring plans to move in the right direction. More importantly, given the inevitable changes that will happen over your tenure, you will have a mechanism to accommodate them in a deliberate and transparent way.

The following sections outline the approach that I have taken to design a target operating model through a number of distinct steps. Adapt them as you see fit to the specifics of your organization, as the functions you require and the specific roles at your organization will vary. Once you have modeled a target organization, I will also describe how this can be used to assess the structure of your existing organization and to create a plan to move toward the modeled one.

ORGANIZATION BY FUNCTIONS OR SERVICES

The first macro activity that you *must* complete is to assess the purpose of your organization and the products or services it delivers. This may sound like a trivial exercise, but in reality this should be carefully considered. The main objective is to understand the functional boundaries that exist between the groups within the organization and their responsibilities for delivering and operating products or services. It is important to have a clear delineation of responsibilities if you expect your leaders to demonstrate unambiguous accountability and ownership. If there are gray areas of responsibility, confusion and accountabilities that no one feels responsible for will result.

As implied, I tend to find it useful to consider the products or services that are being engineered and operated. These could be aligned with functional or infrastructural deliverables, but by assessing the macro organization in this way, you connect to the drivers and success criteria for your organization. What is the alternative to this functional approach, you may ask? In my experience, the technology organizations have often mirrored the business organizations that they support. This does have some advantages—especially in terms of budgetary and stakeholder alignment—but it also introduces some significant issues: duplication and inefficiencies are the biggest, as each team replicates common functions aligned with their specific problems.

As an example, consider a situation where you have two teams: one is responsible for reporting solutions, and the other is responsible for data analytics. These are similar but distinct. The former may be delivering solutions used for financial and customer reports, and the latter may be driving internal business intelligence assessments. Their product portfolios will require the acquisition and provision of necessary data to support their deliverables.

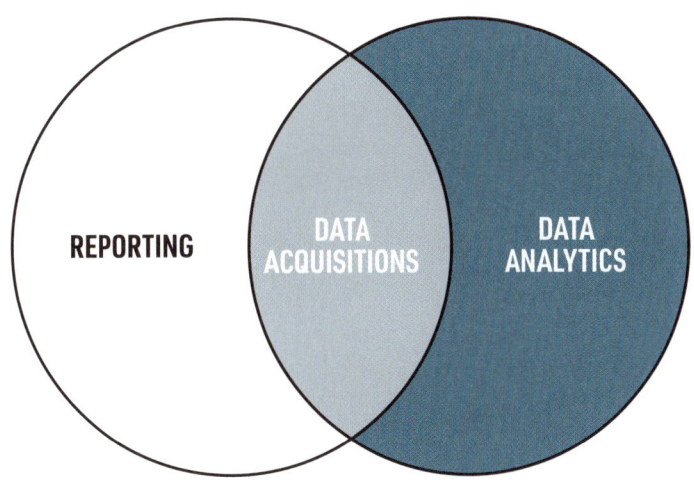

EXAMPLE FUNCTIONAL GROUPS

This duplication is inefficient and creates ambiguity. What if both groups require the same data? Should they both independently source and acquire the data—the easiest solution for them both—or should one group provide the data to the other? The simplest mechanism to create clarity and functional precision is to extract a third group that is wholly responsible for data acquisition and provides those services for consumption by both groups. This provides a number of significant advantages: it consolidates the expense and technical resources in one area, balances investments and priorities from both dependent groups, and promotes reuse of solutions.

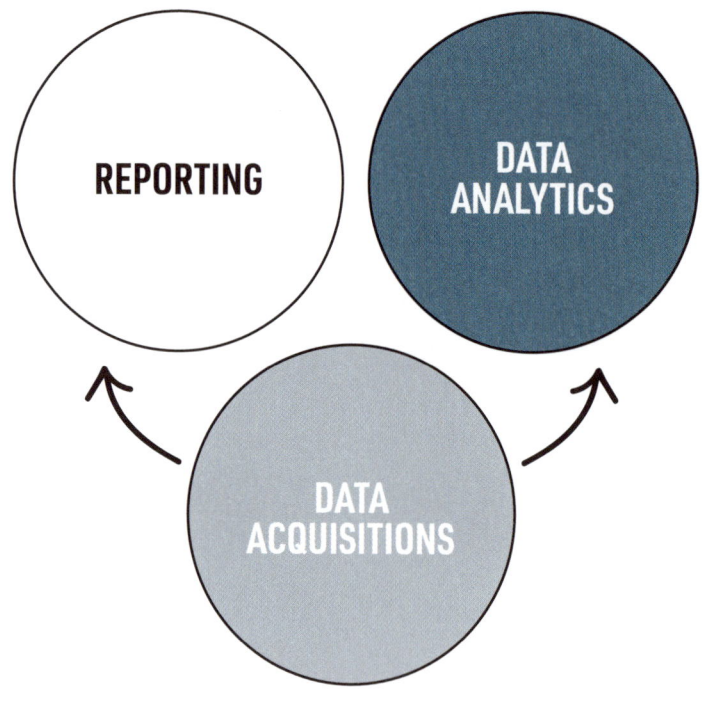

EXTRACTING COMMON FUNCTIONS

A word of caution: This is definitely an exercise of "art over science." Care should be taken to ensure that additional complexity is not introduced through the creation of a myriad of functionally nuanced teams, each of which is interdependent on the others for the provision or consumption of services. Were this the case, nothing would be delivered. It can be beneficial to bundle related functions into the same area, thereby creating a portfolio of synergistic services.

In the example, perhaps a data modeling team is within the same group as the data acquisition team, or AI modeling resides with the data analytics group. It can also be a useful consideration to try to ensure that dependencies only flow in one direction, with one group supporting the others. If that is not possible and there are unavoidable instances in which two groups need to be interdependent on each other, consider placing them in one area under consolidated leadership, which will promote swift conflict resolution.

IDENTIFY NECESSARY ROLES AND SKILLS

Although there may be a great number of diverse functional areas in your organization, it is very likely that the resources they need will have the same or similar skills. If an area requires a project manager or engineer, these same roles will likely be required in other areas. After all, they are all part of a technology organization.

Since you have made your macro assessment of the organization, we now need to make a micro assessment of the individual roles and associated skills that your organization will require. By doing so, we will greatly simplify building the target state organization.

When it comes to describing the types of roles a technology organization may require, there are many nuanced descriptions in use across the industry. For example, developers, software engineers, and programmers are all terms for the individuals who build software products. Perhaps there are subtle differences aligned with these roles, although more likely there is a preference or a prestige that some may associate with one title over another. This is another area where simplification and consistency are important. You must determine the terms for the roles that you require, describe their necessary skills and responsibilities, and adhere to those terms.

After years of refinement, the following are the discrete and simplified types of roles that I use. You may have requirements for other roles, such as risk officers or product managers, but consider these a foundation for your own assessment of necessary roles within your organization:

Engineering: Those who design and develop the software products, agnostic to the language or specific specialization required.

Project Managers: Those who lead the teams that design and develop the software products, agnostic to the methodology being used.

Analysts: Those who understand the stakeholder requirements and translate them to work items. Stakeholders could be external clients or internal groups, such as the information security office.

Quality Assurance: Those who complete various types of testing, such as functional testing, usability testing, and performance testing, to ensure that the software product is of the highest quality.

IT Operations: Those who are responsible for managing the day-to-day activities of an organization's information technology products.

I have no doubt that anyone with a rudimentary understanding of existing technology roles may feel I have left some important roles out. Where are the security analysts and the UX designers? What about DevOps? These are indeed roles that may exist in your organization, but at this stage, where we are modeling a *target state* organization, we do not yet need this level of delineation. The groupings are distinct enough to support simplified modeling and nuanced enough to help understand the broad types of roles that will be required. At the next level, we will create Resource Building Blocks that include details on the specific areas of expertise required.

Within these groupings, there is, however, one distinction that is important to determine: the level of seniority needed for a specific role. At this stage this should be unconstrained. Should your organization already have a number of corporate titles and existing grade levels, I recommend ignoring them for now and only considering *the broad differentiation of responsibilities* that you believe is required. To expand on the previous role groupings, the following are our expanded role groups:

ENGINEERING

Engineering represents the job family that is responsible for the design, development, and testing of software products. All disciplines of engineering are included in this job family, including the development of mobile or front-end applications, full-stack developers, and backend or infrastructure services, leveraging all programming languages. In addition, specialist engineering skills such as "user experience" (a.k.a. UX) and security engineering are also included in this job family.

ENGINEER	SENIOR ENGINEER	PRINCIPAL ENGINEER
An entry-level engineer who contributes to the development of software products (up to five years' experience)	An expert in a given discipline who designs and develops software products and is able to technically lead the development of the products	A specialist in more than one discipline and is able to architect, design, and develop software products

Example engineering roles

PROJECT MANAGER

The project management job family includes all aspects of management activities required to develop a software product. This includes the planning and execution of plans for all sizes and complexity of projects, from small enhancements to enterprise programs. Roles for dedicated project management governance—something that larger regulated enterprises require—are included in this job family.

PROJECT ANALYST	PROJECT MANAGER	PROGRAM MANAGER
An entry-level role that provides project administration and support, such as maintaining project documentation, tracking status, and updating established plans for the assigned project manager	Responsible for the initiation, execution, and completion of technology projects, including scoping and costing projects, monitoring progress, and updating key stakeholders; also responsible for identifying and managing risks and issues identified with the delivery	A senior project manager, who may have responsibility for a portfolio of projects, ensures that cross-collaboration and dependencies are appropriately identified and managed and presides over a number of project managers

Example project manager roles

THE TARGET OPERATING MODEL

ANALYST

The analyst job family includes all dedicated analysis roles, regardless of the specific area of expertise. As such, this includes business analysis, data analysis, security analysis, and application systems analysis. These roles provide specialized expertise that helps bridge the gap to the development teams involved in delivering software products.

ANALYST	SENIOR ANALYST	PRINCIPAL ANALYST
An entry-level analyst who provides support within a specific domain	Responsible for leading analyst activities within a specific specialization to support the development of software products; likely to lead teams of analysts	An expert in one or more domains, responsible for understanding the complexity and risks associated with their domain; may have architectural responsibilities for their domain

Example analyst roles

QUALITY ASSURANCE

The quality assurance job family includes the roles that conduct all aspects of testing of the software product, be it functional, security, performance, or resilience testing. It involves activities and techniques aimed at preventing defects, identifying and resolving issues, and improving overall quality throughout the entire life cycle of the technology product or service.

QA ANALYST	QA LEAD	QA MANAGER
An entry-level role that may be responsible for the execution of established test plans, without necessarily having specialist test domain knowledge	Responsible for the design and execution of test plans, with a specialization in a specific test domain; likely to lead teams of QA analysts	A senior role with expertise in a specific test domain; able to design and monitor complex testing plans that may be required for interdependent projects

Example quality assurance roles

IT OPERATIONS

The IT operations job family includes all roles that are necessary for deployment, hygiene, and operations of the technology product, be it an application or infrastructure. These roles have responsibility for activities such as incident, problem, and change management. This is a far-reaching set of roles. There is a more recent movement to create engineering roles that have operational responsibility, termed DevOps. These types of roles are included in this job family.

ANALYST	SENIOR ANALYST	PRINCIPAL ANALYST
An entry-level analyst who provides support within a specific domain of IT operations, such as help desk or server management	A senior expert in a specific domain of IT operations; able to provide oversight of an IT operations team	A senior expert in IT operations; able to design, execute, and improve the necessary processes and procedures for their domain of expertise; proactive in looking for areas of improvement

Example IT operations roles

These job families provide the fine-grained roles for your organization. Now it will be necessary to create a mechanism to consistently apply them to your target state organizational model. For that, we need to develop a more coarse-grain artifact, the Resource Building Block.

CONSTRUCT RESOURCE BUILDING BLOCKS

As previously described, when designing a technology organization, there will be consistency in the types of roles required. To model a target organization in a consistent and sustainable way and to accommodate the inevitable changes that will occur in a predictable manner, we need to create a more coarse-grained and consistent building block than a role. Without it, each of the functional areas within your organization will very likely inconsistently apply the roles.

The Resource Building Block is a combination of select roles assembled to meet a generalized requirement. These Resource Building Blocks will then be selectively applied to specific functional areas according to their requirements. The combination of all the necessary functional areas will then represent the target state technology organization.

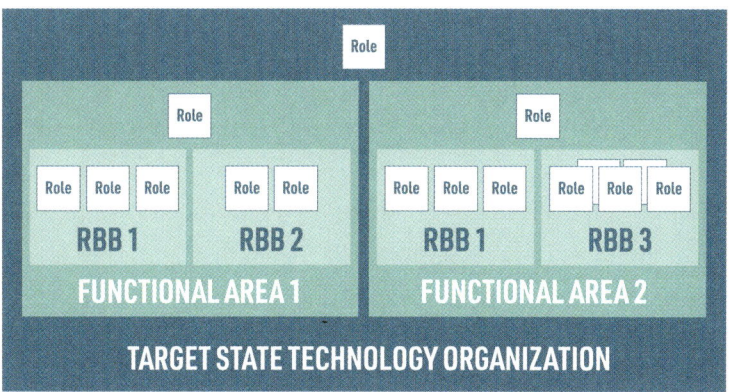

LEVERAGING ROLES, RESOURCES BUILDING BLOCKS, AND FUNCTIONAL AREAS

Although the Resource Building Block is the primary mechanism to build out a specific functional area, it is also acceptable to include specific roles as required, as your teams and functional areas will have individual leadership roles at various levels of the organization.

To create a Resource Building Block, it helps to follow these guidelines:

- First and foremost, the Resource Building Block should be created for a specific job family and, as such, should only include roles from that job family.

- The Resource Building Block is not what we would consider a "team" in the traditional sense, as that would require roles from multiple job families.

- A job family will have a number of specific Resource Building Blocks aligning to the *complexity* or *scale* of the activities for which they will be responsible.

This last guideline is crucial for the Resource Building Blocks to be useful. If we consider the Engineering job family, there are a variety of requirements that will make use of the engineering roles, ranging from the maintenance of simple technology products to designing and developing complex, mission-critical solutions. As such, a number of permutations will be required, and they should align with various levels of complexity undertakings. A representation of these follows:

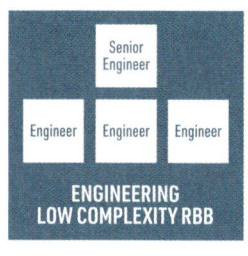
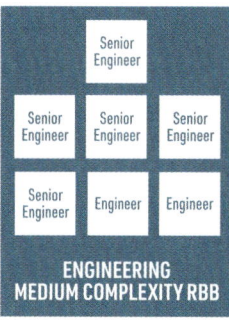
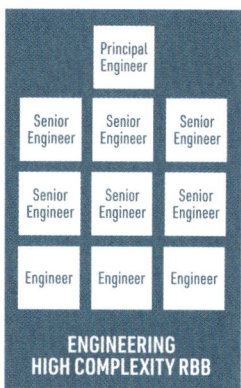

EXAMPLE ENGINEERING RESOURCE BUILDING BLOCKS

As you create the various Resource Building Blocks for a job family, consider specific examples of low, medium, and high complexity use cases to validate the roles needed. There will almost certainly be debate regarding exactly how many roles, and of which level of seniority, will be required. There is no right answer, only the best approximation of what will be required to satisfy the *majority* of use cases. We are trying to model an idealized target state organization, not design for perfection. Remember that these building blocks will be assembled into many different functional areas across your organization.

PUTTING IT ALL TOGETHER

Once you have created sufficient Resource Building Blocks for each of your job families, and considering the different shapes and resourcing needs according to the complexity of the activities that they will address, it is time to map them, and individual roles as required, into the macro functional or service areas that you determined your organization requires.

At this stage, when we map specific Resource Building Blocks into a functional area, we will identify the *specific skills* that are required. Again, job families are by design agnostic to skill types, such as programming languages required, merely providing a grouping of like resources. The Resource Building Block then differentiates the number and level of resources to address specific complexity of problems. For the design of an organization to be meaningful, we do need to understand the specific skills that are required within an assigned functional area.

When, for example, assigning an *Engineering-Low Complexity* Resource Building Block into a functional area that is responsible for building web applications, we may want to identify that the skills required for that block of resources as "JavaScript," or even a specific framework such as "React.js." Conversely, if this were being assigned into an infrastructure team building data services, we may want to identify the skills required as "Java" or "GraphQL." The same applies if there is a need for a specific role that is to be assigned to a functional area.

As we consider the Resource Building Blocks and roles required for a specific functional area in the organization, I strongly recommend recording the reasons for the selection of low, medium, or high complexity Resource Building Blocks, in addition to the specific skills needed. In this way there will be justification and transparency on why the target state organization is laid out the way it is, including what the specific *drivers* for its shape. If in the future the drivers change, then the consequences to the affected areas can be assessed and adjusted.

ENRICHING THE FUNCTIONAL AREAS FOR LOCATION STRATEGY

Once all the functional areas have been designed by applying appropriately sized Resource Building Blocks and specific roles required from the necessary job families, a final enrichment will be to design the *location strategy*. This may not be necessary for smaller organizations, but for medium to large enterprises, especially those operating in multiple cities or countries, it is critical that you consider the most appropriate locations for specific functional areas. Natural synergy with other areas of the firm may dictate where the functional area should be. Likewise, a constraint such as resource availability may determine the most appropriate location. But in every sense, it is important to be deterministic in terms of where a functional team *should* be based. This is a guideline for your future organization, as opposed to you identifying exactly which specific resource will be based where, but it will help you validate the appropriateness of where your existing resources are based.

LEVERAGING THE TARGET STATE ORGANIZATION TO EFFECT CHANGE

If you are fortunate to be working in a "green field" environment and are building out a new organization, then the target state organization that you have modeled should provide a succinct and comprehensible *blueprint* for how to resource your organization. But you will probably inherit an existing organization, with preexisting teams and a preexisting structure. In this situation, the target state organization you design still offers a blueprint or desirable end state, but you will also have a starting point to consider.

Map Existing Staff into the Job Family Roles

When creating Resource Building Blocks, we used the job family role groupings to assemble them, unconstrained by the existing corporate or role titles in your organization. At this stage, as we assess the efficacy of the existing organization, we now need to map your existing roles into the simplified job family groupings.

For example, if you have five existing levels of software developers—say, trainee developer, junior developer, analyst developer, senior analyst developer, and application architect—these need to be mapped into the existing Engineering job family roles—engineer, senior engineer, and principal engineer. These could be represented in the following way:

ENGINEERING JOB FAMILY ROLE	MAPPED EXISTING ROLES
Engineer	Trainee developer and junior developer
Senior engineer	Analyst developer and senior analyst developer
Principal engineer	Application architect

In this way you can categorize your existing staff into the modeled job families, which ultimately allows you to see how close to the target state you are.

Map Existing Teams into the Functional Areas

Your existing teams should be able to be mapped into the Functional Areas. Even if they are currently structured differently, they are nevertheless working toward the same objectives. Some existing teams may not cleanly map to the new modeled functional areas if they provide deliverables to more than one area. Should that be the case, proportion the resources in the existing team to each of the relevant areas.

Assess the Current Organization

At the conclusion of both these mapping exercises, you will be able to calculate existing resources aligned with the new job family roles that would support the newly defined functional areas if you were to move them *today*. This can provide an immediate and useful alignment assessment.

Would you currently have sufficient resources—at the right level of expertise—to support the functions that you require to meet your firm's business objectives? Or conversely, do you have too many resources? Too many junior or senior resources? If you look at your current locations, are the correct resources in the correct locations? It is extremely unlikely that the organization that you have inherited matches the modeled target state organization, but the comparison will show where the gaps exist.

Once you understand these gaps, you can create a plan to drive alignment. As always, it is critical that your plan takes the operational risks that change may introduce into account. Remember, your existing teams are currently delivering products and supporting their business areas. You do not want to introduce disruptive changes or manifest unacceptable levels of operational risk.

A number of phases will likely be required to safely migrate toward your target state. Even then, given that the target state represents an unconstrained view, you should also recognize whether there are tangible constraints that compromise your ability to attain that target state. Perhaps resources are required in a given location for business or regulatory reasons. Whatever the reason, the validity of these constraints must be challenged and verified, as you do not want to propagate historic constraints that may no longer be valid.

This comparison of the existing organization to the modeled target state may provide one other significant benefit, depending on what it reveals. If the current organization is overresourced or too geographically dispersed, then you can make a benefits case on rationalizing the organization, including associated savings. Conversely, if the organization is underresourced, then an investment case can be made. Either way, this nuanced level of evidence and precision will help make a compelling case.

CHAPTER 12

MANAGING RISK

If you don't invest in risk management, it doesn't matter what business you're in—it's a risky business.
—GARY COHN

I am fortunate to have spent the majority of my career operating in a highly regulated industry, with extensive regulatory and legal expectations and comprehensive risk management processes. Within the financial services industry, this protects the client, the firm, and indeed the whole industry from catastrophic failures of controls, systems, and processes.

I have always considered the regulatory oversight merely a means of enforcing appropriate behaviors and actions that *should already be taking place*. It has surprised me that, in many other less regulated industries, the same rigor in risk management is seldom applied. Do other industries face less risk of a cyber or a ransomware attack? Does adverse impact to the clients or firms matter less? Is organizational resilience unimportant? I would posit that all these things matter equally, regardless of the industry and the level of regulatory oversight your firm operates in.

As the CTO, it is your responsibility to define, quantify, and manage your firm's technology risks, regardless of the regulatory expectations. To achieve this, it is important to comprehend what exactly falls within the scope of technology risk. Technology is increasingly the crux of most businesses, so understanding your specific responsibilities as the CTO—versus the CISO, COO, or CEO—is extremely important. Risks must be actively managed by accountable and empowered owners if there is to be risk reduction and appropriate risk acceptance.

DEFINING TECHNOLOGY RISK

Technology risk is usually considered a subcomponent of operational risk, which covers any event that affects your organization's ability to operate. Technology risk specifically includes information technology risks that may negatively affect business operations. This could cover a range of scenarios, including software failures, concentration risks with specific vendors or suppliers, or even basic power outages.

A number of robust risk management frameworks have been developed to help define and manage technology risks. I have found two key frameworks, both defined by the *Information Systems Audit and Control Association (ISACA)*,[43] to be extremely useful: the *Risk IT Framework* and the *Control Objectives for Information and Related Technology (COBIT)*.[44]

The ISACA Risk IT Framework provides a comprehensive definition of technology risk, including the following three fundamental risk categories:

IT Benefit / Value Enablement Risk: Where risks arise when the technology does not meet the business requirements, is misaligned with enterprise IT strategy, or introduces defects or design flaws, leading to insufficient enablement of business functions, products, and services.

IT Program / Project Delivery Risk: Where risks arise from a failure to achieve the planned outcomes from a project and lead to failure in the delivery of required products, services, or capabilities—including controls—in a timely manner.

IT Operations and Service Delivery Risk: Where risks arise from degraded performance of technology processes, assets, and services to a level that is insufficient to support business functions, products, and services.

Interestingly, cybersecurity risk is often considered a subcomponent of technology risk—even in the *Cyber and Information Security Risk* section of the ISACA Risk IT Framework. I do not agree with this position. Although many of the same controls may help address cybersecurity risks, and most certainly the same technology assets may be within scope for assessment, in my opinion the appetite for technology risk should be judged separately from a firm's cybersecurity risk appetite.

As an example, the need to ensure that machines are appropriately patched is important for both technology *and* cybersecurity risk. If a machine's software is *not* patched properly, it may not operate correctly because of defects or bugs addressed in later versions of the software. From a technological perspective, there may be impact, but perhaps that impact is tolerable. Yet from a cybersecurity perspective, those same defects may represent weaknesses in security controls. Ensuring that the software is up to date is thus of *critical* importance. In other words, what may be considered medium risk from a technology perspective might be a major risk from a cybersecurity perspective.

I also believe that sufficient cybersecurity resources and activities exist for cybersecurity risk to be assessed independently, including those that take place within a security operations center. The consequence of cybersecurity being out of risk appetite is reason enough for it to be considered a peer of technology risk.

To quantify risk, we need to be able to group and categorize the risks. For the highest level of grouping, I use the three risk categories that the ISACA Risk IT Framework provides. This is still quite coarse-grained and needs to be broken down further. When we assess systemic risk failure, we should group items in a way that helps us clearly identify which areas need our attention.

The second framework, the ISACA COBIT 2019 Framework, exists to help firms mange risks by helping identify areas with control requirements. Fundamentally, it defines the components necessary to build a governance system, including the necessary principles, design factors, and objectives, *without* prescribing the technical framework or specifics required. It also distinguishes between required governance oversight and the management activities. It is a well-established and robust set of materials, developed over the past fifty or so years, that I would recommend exploring. Nonetheless, my use with regard to managing technology risk is solely to leverage the management components to create an appropriate subclassification of *Risk Objectives* that is aligned with specific control objectives.

Reference: *COBIT 2019 Framework - Introduction and Methodology, Chapter 4 Basic Concepts: Governance and Components, Figure 4.2*

EDM01 - Ensured Governance Framework Setting and Maintenance	EDM02 - Ensured Benefits Delivery	EDM03 - Ensured Risk Optimization	EDM04 - Ensured Resource Optimization	EDM05 - Ensured Stakeholder Engagement		
					MEA01 - Managed Performance and Conformance Monitoring	MEA02 - Managed System of Internal Control
					MEA03 - Managed Compliance with External Requirements	MEA04 - Managed Assurance
AP001 - Managed I&T Management Framework	AP002 - Managed Strategy	AP003 - Managed Enterprise Architecture	AP004 - Managed Innovation	AP005 - Managed Portfolio	AP006 - Managed Budget and Costs	AP007 - Managed Human Resources
AP008 - Managed Relationships	AP009 - Managed Service Agreements	AP010 - Managed Vendors	AP011 - Managed Quality	AP012 - Managed Risk	AP014 - Managed Data	AP013 - Managed Security
BAI01 - Managed Programs	BAI02 - Managed Requirements Definition	BAI03 - Managed Solutions Identification and Build	BAI04 - Managed Availability and Capacity	BAI05 - Managed Organizational Change	BAI06 - Managed IT Changes	BAI07 - Managed IT Change Acceptance and Transitioning
BAI08 - Managed Knowledge	BAI09 - Managed Assets	BAI10 - Managed Configuration	BAI11 - Managed Projects			
DSS01 - Managed Operations	DSS02 - Managed Service Requests and Incidents	DSS03 - Managed Continuity	DSS04 - Managed Problems	DSS05 - Managed Security Services	DSS06 - Managed Business Process Controls	

COBIT 2019 FRAMEWORK INTRODUCTION AND METHODOLOGY-BASIC COMPONENTS
REPRINTED WITH PERMISSION FROM ISACA© 2018 ISACA.

MANAGING RISK

COBIT 2019 details forty distinct objectives with five objectives related specifically to governance activities and thirty-five related to management activities. For the purpose of further classifying risk, it is the management objectives that are the most useful. Not all thirty-five are required verbatim to help classify technology risk. We can group related items to create a simplified view. Given that technology risk needs to be well understood at all levels of an organization, the simpler that we can convey these risk objectives, the more likely that there will be broad comprehension and clarity by the risk stakeholders. As such, the following represents a simplified set of risk objectives for each of the categories.

IT Benefit / Value Enablement

This area predominantly relates to the technology activities and processes that develop and build *new* solutions. The following are the risk objectives that I would propose, including a reference to the relevant ISACA COBIT 2019 management objectives:

> **Requirements and Solutions Development:** Combines *BAI02 Manage Requirements Definition* and *BAI03 Manage Solutions Identification and Build*. From a management perspective, there will be processes for requirement definition that are separate and distinct from those related to designing and building the solution. From a risk perspective, both fall under "development" or software development life cycle risk, so for simplification and clarity, they can be combined.
>
> **Architecture:** Given the richer description of architecture in this book, this subsumes *APO03 Manage Enterprise Architecture*; otherwise, it would suggest only the activities associated with the Enterprise Level of architecture.

Change Acceptance: This is a slightly simpler description for *BAI07 Manage IT Change Acceptance and Transitioning*, which covers the activities required to review and approve changes to live systems or processes.

As is hopefully apparent, these risk objectives cover activities related to designing, building, and deploying new software applications and services *before* being applied into the live systems or production environment.

IT Operations / Service Delivery

This area relates to the activities and processes necessary to operate the *existing* technology solutions that support your firm. Many distinct activities occur for that to be successful, so a number of risk objectives are thus required here. The following are the ones that I would propose, again including a reference to the relevant ISACA COBIT 2019 management objectives:

Manage Third-Party Relationships: Combines *APO08 Manage Relationships, APO09 Manage Service Agreements*, and *APO10 Manage Vendors*, all of which predominantly relate to dealing with third parties. This happens often in running technology solutions, as third-party solution providers can be used to complete dedicated activities such as help desks or systems administration activities. Likewise, vendors will provide many of the software and hardware products that your firm will procure and leverage. It is important to understand the risks that this may introduce to your firm, given you will have less direct control over these activities.

Manage IT Assets: Combines *BAI09 Manage Assets* and

BAI10 Manage Configurations. These activities provide an inventory on the various IT assets, including software and hardware, and the base configurations required to ensure they are appropriately secured.

Availability and Capacity: Analogous to *BAI04 Manage Availability and Capacity.* Capacity management covers the activities that ensure there is sufficient capacity for the services being executed, such as monitoring whether there is sufficient space in a database. Availability management also covers activities to ensure that services are accessible when needed. There may be distinct processes to complete both these activities, but they relate to each other. For example, when a database runs out of space and data can no longer be stored, it may then have a direct consequence on the availability of the services that create and store that data.

IT Service Management (ITSM): There are distinct processes involved in managing incidents, problems, and change, with all three considered the bedrock for ITSM. Incident management covers the activities that occur when an event in your production environment could cause a detrimental impact, as well as the steps necessary to restore services to normal. Problem management is concerned with understanding the root cause of incidents and identifying thematic challenges. IT change management ensures that changes are made into your production environment without causing disruption and outages. All three, although distinct, relate to one another. As such, we can combine *DSS02 Manage Service Requests and Incidents*, *DSS02 Manage Problems*, and *BAI06 Manage IT Change* when considering the associated risks.

Manage Continuity: This is an area that could be combined with availability and capacity as both pertain to the availability of business activities. However, continuity tends to be a more holistic set of procedures to enable the recovery of business services in the event of a significant event or disaster. This may entail establishing alternative technology solutions or manual processes to ensure the continuation of business services, something that can incur significant cost. As such, it is normal for only the critical business services—that is, those deemed core to delivering your services to clients. This is analogous to *DSS04 Manage Continuity*.

Data Management: This is a subset of the activities associated with *APO14 Manage Data*, which includes all activities related to Data Governance, classification, quality, and Data Management. From a pure technology risk perspective, the most important thing here is Data Management: how data is created, stored, and protected. The other governance activities, although important for your firm to complete, do not directly relate to technology risk.

It may be beneficial to your firm, perhaps as a result of having immature processes in any of the areas that I have combined, to have distinct risk objectives, disaggregating the ones that I have combined. In this way there will be clarity on exactly which IT operations and service delivery processes are introducing risks and require attention.

IT Program / Project Delivery Risk

Whereas the prior two classifications effectively cover the activities to create *new* technology assets and to operate the *existing* ones, this area covers the activities required to manage the associated programs and projects common to both of the other areas. The following is the only risk objective that I would propose, again including a reference to the relevant ISACA COBIT 2019 management objectives:

> **Manage Programs and Projects:** Combines *BAI01 Manage Programs* and *BAI11 Manage Projects*. The variations between these activities are predominantly driven by the scale of the initiative being completed. A program will be a portfolio of related projects, and from a risk perspective, there is little difference between programs and projects. While programs can be more complex and inherently of greater consequence when they fail, in my experience, a specific project *within* a program tends to be the most common cause of broader failure.

One item to note: Some form of project management will likely occur in the nontechnology areas of your firm, whether that is cybersecurity, real estate, or operations. It seems obvious, but it is worth noting that only programs and projects within scope for inclusion here are those that relate to technology.

Unmapped COBIT 2019 Management Activities

It may seem as though I have missed some key management objectives, such as *APO04 Manage Innovation* or *APO06 Manage Budget or Costs*. Remember, while these objectives are all necessary for the successful management of an IT organization (unsurprisingly, as that is the intent of the framework), that does not necessarily mean they are all quantifiable or significant in terms of impact for the *management of technology risk*. If you fail to innovate and incorporate new technology, you may be at a competitive disadvantage (and failing as a CTO), but operationally, this does not significantly affect *your risk profile.*

If you have incidents or failures as a direct result of the ITSM process, then you almost certainly are affecting your risk profile (and again failing as a CTO). In a similar fashion, *APO13 Manage Security* and *DSS05 Manage Security Services* could form part of the definition of cybersecurity risk, but again, I believe that should be distinguished and separated from technology risk. Of course, the above is my guidance only; you should determine the most relevant risk classifications for your firm, as this is again an area that is "more art than science."

QUANTIFYING RISK

When determining how best to quantify technology risk, it is important that your approach is both easy to understand and idempotent—that is, whether assessed now or later over the same period, the result remains the same. For credible risk management, it is important that both improvements and deterioration within your risk profile can be directly attributed to the items being assessed, not as a result of inconsistencies in the way items are being measured or unexpected changes to the methodology. To meet this objective and ensure a consistent mechanism to quantify risk, I believe in using both quantitative and qualitative assessments.

Quantitative and Qualitative Assessments

The quantitative assessment is, as you would imagine, one based on measurements or *key control indicators (KCIs)* that accurately capture and reflect the effectiveness of a specific control. Why focus on controls? *Because risks are mitigated by effective controls.*

By measuring the effectiveness or ineffectiveness of a control, we can infer the remaining residual risk.

The qualitative assessment is one that is based on other risk factors you must consider to have a comprehensive view of overall technology risk. Why is this required when we already have a robust quantitative assessment? For one, there may be emerging risks for which controls do not yet exist. These may manifest in other ways, whether through operational losses or audit assessments, so it is important to incorporate them.

Interestingly, the quantitative assessment may provide *leading risk* indicators. Over time you can track the changes to the indicator, whether those changes are degradations or improvements. The qualitative assessment tends to be a *lagging risk* indicator, as the items it turns up often do so after the risk has materialized—for example, after recording an operational loss or an audit assessment has been completed.

Risk Tolerance Statements

We need a mechanism to collate both these quantitative and qualitative assessments together, and the best mechanism for the job is *risk tolerance statements*. These describe your firm's appetite for a specific area of risk *within a specific risk objective*. They provide a concise and bounded description of the risk appetite, expressed in plain language. Having a simple statement of risk tolerance and the ability to communicate whether you are operating within it is a powerful and concise tool for engaging with senior stakeholders.

For example, we may state within our risk objective of *IT Service Management* that we have "a low tolerance for outages as a direct result of the IT change process." Subsequently, we may establish a related quantitative assessment by establishing a number of KCIs.

One example could be a measure of the number of outages that were a direct result of a failure to follow the prescribed IT change process in a given period, such as the following:

$$\% \text{ IT Change Failure} = \text{\# of outages with a root cause of change process failure} / \text{\# total number of changes in a <period>}$$

Of course, we first need an appropriate threshold to represent a "low tolerance" for this indicator to be effective. The best way to do this is to simply measure the indicator over a period. Once you determine a level that represents being "in breach," you can then create a *warning threshold* that indicates whether a KCI is moving toward being in breach. For the quantitative assessment, the tolerance statement would be deemed out of appetite if the majority of the associated KCIs were in breach of their thresholds.

In a similar fashion, we can establish qualitative assessments. For example, were an audit to identify systemic weaknesses in the IT change process itself, the audit findings would be a qualitative assessment that could also be mapped to the *same* tolerance statement.

Recognizing that we now have a number of considerations when assessing a specific risk tolerance statement, the following order of precedence should be applied:

1. First, validate all *quantitative* KCIs associated to a specific tolerance statement. If the majority are in breach of their thresholds, then the tolerance statement is out of appetite, and no other assessment is needed.
2. If the KCIs show that you are operating within appetite,

then evaluate the qualitative assessments for the tolerance statement. If they indicate a breach, then the tolerance statement is out of appetite.

It is important to note that the qualitative assessment can *only move you out of appetite*. They cannot be used to move a tolerance statement back to risk appetite if the quantitative assessment has already indicated that it is out of appetite. This is a conservative approach and ensures that your assessment is indeed idempotent and explainable.

If a qualitative assessment could move you into appetite, then there would be no benefit in the quantitative assessment. This is ultimately the key facet of the *explainability* of the risk. For this reason, if a new tolerance statement is introduced for which there is not yet any quantitative assessment, I would strongly recommend that it is assumed to be *out* of appetite until such time as a quantitative assessment can demonstrate that it is *within* appetite.

One final point on risk tolerance statements: Once established, they should not be volatile. There should only be changes to them if there are significant changes to a firm's business objectives or appetite for risk.

Materiality—Likelihood and Impact Assessments

I strongly recommend measuring more than one KCI for a specific tolerance statement as part of the quantitative risk assessment. This ensures that multiple data points are considered when the risk assessment is being made. However, not all KCIs will be equally impactful to the tolerance statement. Recognize that using a simple majority, the assessment may not truly reflect the associated risks.

Accommodations must be made to cater for these differences.
One mechanism to do this is to gauge the *risk materiality* of the indicator being measured. A simple but effective means of doing this is to leverage a risk assessment matrix[45], which was first developed in the Electronic System Center, US Air Force. The materiality of a risk may be assessed by looking at the *impact* or severity of the consequences that a failure of the control would have, as well as the *likelihood* or probability of that failure. Although these assessments are qualitative in nature, they are simple to understand. If you apply them consistently, they will provide a concise assessment of the materiality of the risk that the indicator is measuring.

Let's explore how these might be determined for KCIs.

- The **Impact** could be derived by considering the impact to the client, the potential financial losses that may result, the negative consequence to the firm's reputation or brand, or perhaps the potential for regulatory actions.

- The **Likelihood** is derived by considering the likelihood of an impact occurring if the control fails while also considering other compensations or mitigations that may be in place.

For both, a simple three-by-three matrix can be established to determine materiality by looking at the intersection of both Impact and Likelihood. The greater the impact and the higher the likelihood, the greater the materiality of the risk.

As an example, let's consider a KCI that measures the completeness of the software patching of firewalls. As the firewalls are providing network controls, ensuring protection against application-layer attacks and malware, this would probably be assessed as having High Impact were it not completed (or, more accurately, if the threshold of completeness was not met).

However, the likelihood of impact may be deemed to be Unlikely, as numerous compensating controls exist in addition to the security that the firewall provides. For example, there could be network segmentation in place or intrusion prevention systems to prevent network security attacks. As a result, the materiality of this indicator would be Moderate Risk (3): High Impact (3) × Unlikely (1).

IMPACT / LIKELIHOOD	LOW IMPACT (SCORE 1)	MODERATE IMPACT (SCORE 2)	HIGH IMPACT (SCORE 3)
UNLIKELY (SCORE 1)	VERY LOW RISK (1 x 1=1)	LOW RISK (1 x 2=2)	MODERATE RISK (1 x 3=3)
LIKELY (SCORE 2)	LOW RISK (2 x 1=2)	MEDIUM RISK (2 x 2=4)	HIGH RISK (2 x 3=6)
HIGHLY LIKELY (SCORE 3)	MODERATE RISK (3 x 1=3)	HIGH RISK (2 x 3=6)	MAJOR RISK (3 x 3=9)

RISK MATERIALITY THREE-BY-THREE ASSESSMENT

The above provides a simple example of a three-by-three matrix, whereas in practice, it may be deemed necessary to expand either axis to create a more fine-grained materiality assessment.

Weightings

As previously stated, a simple majority of KCIs being in breach is probably not nuanced enough to reflect whether a specific tolerance statement is truly out of appetite. As we now have materiality assessments for each indicator, we can use them to construct a mechanism for weighting different indicators and the consequences of breaching a specific tolerance statement.

As an example, let's envision a tolerance statement that has three associated KCIs. The specifics are not important, but let us assume that one of the indicators is assessed as a Major Risk, one is High Risk, and the last is Moderate Risk. Looking at the risk assessment matrix on the previous page, these each had a number associated with them—nine for the Major Risk, six for the High Risk, and three for the Moderate Risk. By adding these together, we can state that the tolerance statement has a total risk weighting denominator of eighteen.

Now when we complete our quantitative assessment, we can use this weighting to determine the consequence of each being in breach or not. We can still state that the tolerance statement is out of appetite if the majority of the *weighted* indicators remain in breach. If we assume that the Moderate and High Risk indicators are in breach, it meets the previously defined simple majority and meets the new weighted criteria as follows:

$$High\ Risk\ Weighting + Moderate\ Risk\ Weighting\ /$$
$$Total\ Risk\ Weighting >= 50\%$$

or

$$(6 + 3) / 18 * 100 >= 50\%$$

If we now to assume that only the Major Risk indicator is in breach, this would not meet our simple majority assessment, as it is only one of three metrics, but it *does* meet the weighted assessment:

> Major Risk Weighting / Total Weighting >= 50%

or

> 9 / 18 * 100 >= 50%

Given that this one indicator represents a Major Risk, it is appropriate that when it is in breach, the tolerance statement itself is considered out of appetite. The more key indicators associated with a specific tolerance statement, the more nuanced the quantitative assessment will be. At the very least, you should ensure that there is more than one associated to each tolerance statement and ideally three or more.

REPORTING RISK

Even when considering the comparatively transparent and evidence-based assessment of risk, it is important to simplify further to ensure clarity and acceptance of the risk assessment. Explanations of the nuance of a specific risk tolerance statement or the relevance of specific quantitative assessments will not be productive or useful.

Luckily, the hierarchical nature of this risk framework makes reporting technology risk comparatively straightforward. It is like the engine warning indicators that come standard in most cars, which are connected to a plethora of specific monitoring systems across the vehicle. If you see that the indicator is on, you know there is an issue, even if specifics are unknown. If you are sensible, you will take your car to a garage, where a mechanic will use their equipment to look at the specific sensors to diagnose the issue, then put forward a plan to fix the problem.

In a similar fashion, the overall technology risk assessment is derived by aggregating the risks associated with the three categories of risk. Each of these consists of one or more risk objectives, which, in turn, have a number of risk tolerance statements. Each risk tolerance statement has a number of weighted KCIs assessed as part of the quantitative assessment, which ultimately determine whether the tolerance statement is within appetite. Finally, a qualitative assessment may be applied to override the quantitative assessment if other factors are deemed to be significant and relevant.

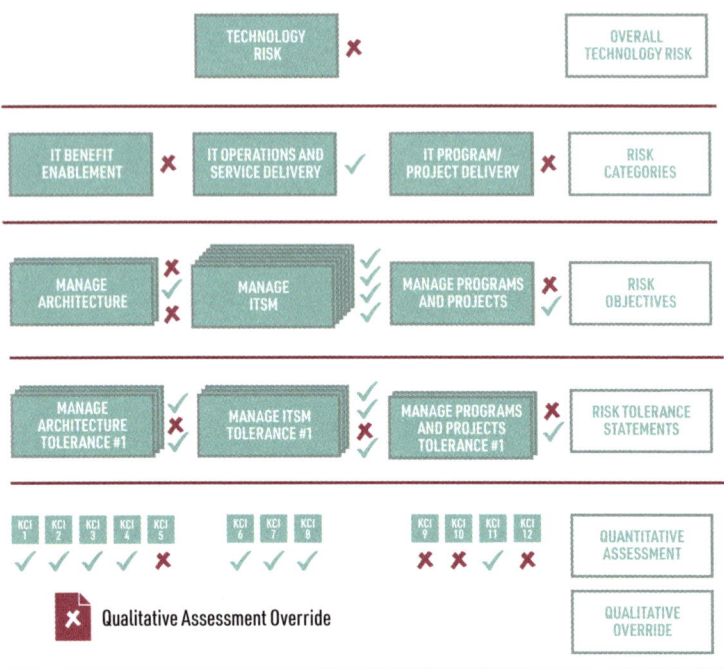

AN AGGREGATED VIEW OF TECHNOLOGY RISK REPORTING

The diagram above illustrates this relationship and the ability to report risks at the various levels, which is useful, depending on the audience that you are communicating with. In this simplified example, technology risk could be considered out of appetite, as the *IT Benefit / Value Enablement* and *IT Program / Project Delivery* risk categories are out of appetite as a consequence of several of their risk objectives being out of appetite. Despite the quantitative assessment for the related tolerance statements being acceptable in the instance of *Manage Architecture*, a qualitative override has been applied to move it out of appetite.

An Example of a Risk Dashboard

Rather than assessing the risk at the level of three risk categories, it is more precise to assess it at the level of the risk objectives, which should be of equal importance. Given my suggested ten distinct risk objectives across the three categories, I would suggest that if half or greater are out of appetite, then overall the technology risk would be considered out of appetite.

RISK OBJECTIVE	TOLERANCE STATEMENTS	QUANTITATIVE ASSESSMENT			CURRENT QUALITATIVE ASSESSMENT	OVERALL RISK ASSESSMENT
		CURRENT - 1 MONTH	CURRENT - 2 MONTHS	CURRENT - MONTH		
IT BENEFIT/VALUE ENABLEMENT						
Requirements & Solutions Development	3	✗	✗	✗		✓
Architecture	3				Failed Audit	✗
Change Acceptance	3	✗	✗			✓
IT OPERATIONS/SERVICE DELIVERY						
Manage Third-Party Relationships	6	✗		✗		
Manage IT Assets	4					✓
Availability & Capacity	3	✗	✗	✗		✗
IT Service Management	11					✓
Manage Continuity	3			✗		✗
Data Management	0				No Quantitative Assessment	✗
IT PROGRAM/PROJECT DELIVERY						
Manage Programs & Projects	5				Failed Audit	✗

A simple risk dashboard can be created to provide comprehensive risk status, as shown. In this example, there are a few items to note, including the following:

- The ten Risk Objectives are shown grouped according to their Risk Classification.

- Each Risk Objective has a number that shows how many Risk Tolerance Statements are associated with it, with appropriate KCIs in place.

- The Quantitative Assessment shows the current month and the two prior months. This is useful to show momentum and whether the risk posture is degrading or improving.

- The *Requirements and Solutions Development* has three associated Risk Tolerance Statements. Withi1 the quantitative assessment, which shows the status of the associated KCIs, we can see that some of the KCIs are currently in breach—the green and red box—but overall the Quantitative Risk assessment is within tolerance.

- There is a similar situation with *Manage Third-Party Relationships*, but in this case, the overall risk assessment is in warning, as sufficient KCIs are in breach.

- Both *Architecture* and *Manage Program and Projects* are in appetite according to their quantitative assessment, but a qualitative override has been applied due to failed Audits in both case, which has resulted in classifying both Risk Objectives as out of appetite.

- *Data Management* has no Risk Tolerance statements with

appropriate KCIs in place, and as such, is immediately considered to be out of appetite.

- Overall, five of the ten Risk Objectives are out of appetite for various reasons. This meets the 50 percent threshold, so technology risk would be considered out of appetite.

THE IMPORTANCE OF INDEPENDENT RISK CHALLENGE

Having worked within the financial services industry for the majority of my technology career, I am familiar with and find great comfort operating within what is termed the *Three Lines of Defense* model. It was defined by the Institute of Internal Auditors (IIA)[46] and aims to provide clarity on the necessary roles that ensure effective risk management and internal governance.

The model broadly defines three lines of defense that coordinate and collaborate to ensure that organizational objectives are met within acceptable risk tolerance levels. From a risk management perspective, these lines provide the following accountabilities:

First Line Management is responsible for the ownership of risks associated with daily activities and the associated controls that must be maintained.

Second Line Supervision is responsible for the oversight of the First Line, including ownership of risk policies and ensuring they are appropriately applied.

Third Line Assurance is responsible for the independent assessment of the efficacy and effectiveness of both the First and Second Lines.

This model is widely acknowledged and implemented by a number of industries. Should this not be the case for your firm, let me reiterate the importance of the second line roles and responsibilities as they pertain to risk management. As detailed in the *Three Lines of Defense* model paper of IIA, the second line is responsible for "*the development, implementation, and continuous improvement of risk management practices (including internal control) at a process, systems, and entity level. [Ensuring] the achievement of risk management objectives, such as: compliance with laws, regulations, and acceptable ethical behavior; internal control; information and technology security; sustainability; and quality assurance.*" The second line above all provides expertise, monitoring, and challenge on risk-related matters.

When considering this approach to technology risk management, which relies on a number of subjective assessments, *independent* challenge is important to ensure accuracy and consistency. This is true when evaluating the materiality of the key indicators within the quantitative assessment and assessing the impact of relevant qualitative factors.

PART IV
LEADERSHIP

CHAPTER 13

BEING A LEADER, NOT A MANAGER

If your actions inspire others to dream more, learn more, do more, and become more, you are a leader.

–JOHN QUINCY ADAMS

The CTO is the preeminent technology leader within a firm, and success in the role absolutely depends on being an effective leader. This starts by creating a strong and compelling technology vision for what you want to achieve as the CTO and, perhaps more importantly, how you want to achieve it. Why is the *how* as or more important than the *what*? I firmly believe that sustainable success flows from establishing a culture and ethos that will cascade through your senior leadership team. There must be comprehension and buy-in to what you want to achieve. If the culture is wrong, then execution will be significantly harder.

As a leader, I always try to identify individuals in my leadership team who will operate and lead as I expect, operating with my values and principles. The old adages of "One bad apple spoils the barrel" and "The fish rots from the head" are both apt here. It only takes one cynical leader, one dissenting or negative outlook, to hinder success or, worse, lead to failure.

To be clear, I am not looking for yes-men. I seek those individuals who will constructively challenge and enrich our team and who demonstrate accountability and complete ownership. I firmly believe in the one-plus-one-equals-three effect, where the sum is greater than its constituent parts. A strong leadership team that can cooperate with the values and principles that you outline as a leader will collectively deliver much more than they—or you—can alone.

There are already plenty of great resources available on leadership in general. I'm here to share certain beneficial aspects of *technology* leadership that I have assimilated over my career. I am not trying to present a definitive approach that everyone must follow for success, only the leadership tenets that have been beneficial to me. Take from it the parts that work for you and add to it as you see fit.

LEADERSHIP VALUES

When I join a new organization, I usually convey my values early in a town hall–style forum. This happens before I attempt to establish my technology vision and supporting strategies and even before I start assessing my incumbent leadership team. I believe it is important that my teammates understand my values from the start. Most are expressed as single sentences that are easy to understand and remember, concisely describing traits that I truly value and that have served me well at many different firms.

- *Thinking is cheap; doing gets expensive quickly:* It is important to complete just enough analysis to be sure you are heading in the right direction. If you don't know where you're going, you'll get nowhere fast. Too often, there is excessive motion in the *doing* before there is sufficient comprehension of the task at hand, resulting in mistakes and miscomprehension that require rework.

- **Understand and focus on the outcomes, not the activities:** All too often, teams get caught up in their activities and reporting on what they are doing, the minutiae of their actions, instead of understanding which outcomes and objectives have been delivered or not. The latter is of much greater value and should be celebrated in turn.

- **Appreciate what it takes to be successful, not the reasons why something won't be:** Naysayers will quickly tell you all kinds of things that will impede your success. It's more constructive to pivot away from that and toward what needs to be addressed to be successful.

- **Challenge each other but always with respect:** Collaboration and teamwork are key, and challenges at all levels of any organization must be facilitated and treated with respect. An absence of any challenge can be a sign of passive-aggressive behavior, which is one of the most destructive impediments to success, often leading to delays and dysfunction.

- **Propose solutions; do not pass along problems:** Even if resolution resides elsewhere, be proactive in helping others to the fullest extent possible. I used to use the phrase "If you find it, fix it," but this can have the negative consequence that the wrong group may feel obliged to own the wrong problems.

- *Deliver what our customers need, not what they say they want:* Hopefully what a client wants is indeed what they need, but never assume that this is the case. First, understand their objectives and validate their asks. A trusted advisor will steer their customers toward solutions that truly address their needs, not their wants.

- *Take ownership but escalate issues early:* Demonstrating ownership doesn't mean you cannot ask for help or escalate issues. That transparency is important to build trust and demonstrate that the delegation was appropriate. As a result, issues will be recognized and resolved in a timely fashion.

- *Create sustainable strategic solutions over tactical time-to-market ones:* The "quick win" is often exactly that. Rarely is the quickest solution the best solution. Yes, there will be times when a tactical solution is needed, but that decision should be weighed against what the *right* solution would be.

- *Find what you can reuse, not what you want to build:* Technologists understandably love to build new things. I know I did! You should recognize and reward those teams who set out to leverage what is already in use—there will be less risk and cost in them doing so.

- *Report on the outstanding items and risks, not the just the completed items:* Successful outcomes should be celebrated, but I care even more about what's going to impede future success and where outstanding delivery risk remains.

LEADERSHIP PRINCIPLES

In my experience, there are several fundamental leadership principles that can greatly improve your chances of success in meeting the core objectives of your role. Think of these as the overarching code of conduct. They should underpin any activities or actions you take. Not every principle will apply to every situation, but they are important to keep in the back of your mind.

Beyond Committed

You must establish a compelling technology vision and realize it through the development of concise and connected strategies that are easily understood and executed by your organization. But beyond their content, complete conviction in what you are trying to achieve is of even greater importance. It is incredibly important to simply convey energy. Long before there is a strong comprehension of what you are trying to achieve, your team, your organization, and indeed the whole firm will need to recognize that you will be driving them with focus and certitude toward realizing your technology vision. If you are not genuinely excited, why should they be? If you have full conviction on your path, you will, without a doubt, be excited and beyond committed.

Ensure Transparency and Inclusiveness in All Processes and Decision-Making

It is human nature to challenge and question what is not understood. The more inclusive you can be in engaging key participants, whether in the development of core processes or resolution of key decisions, the less likely people will be to reject them outright. To be absolutely clear, I am not advocating for decisions to be made by committee—these are usually destined to fail. I am simply encouraging transparency and active engagement. Ensure that participants feel accountability for their decisions and that their perspectives and concerns have been heard. As the leader, you will ultimately make the final decision, but others should comprehend the constraints and drivers that led you to make them.

All Activities Must Enable the Realization of Strategic Objectives

Every action you take should accelerate and simplify the attainment of your firm's strategic objectives. This could include simplifying the deliverables for your technical teams or providing conciseness and transparency regarding the efficacy of strategic deliverables for senior management. It seems obvious, but I have observed many occasions where a procedure or standard's rationale has long since been forgotten or is simply no longer relevant. Yet rather than decommissioning or eliminating it, it somehow persists and has continued to be propagated. Why? Usually there is a team or group responsible for executing that procedure, and rarely do those folks voluntarily eliminate their roles. For better or worse, that's your responsibility.

Embrace Change

One aspect of technology that is undoubtedly inevitable is that there will always be innovation and new products, techniques, and approaches introduced. As the CTO, you must accept this reality and accommodate these changes while ensuring that risk oversight and returns on investments are also considered. New does not necessarily mean better; it just means new.

In my career, there have been new innovations and inventions that have completely changed my approach to delivering solutions and managing technology: the move from mainframes to client-server, then client-server to n-tier architectures, the onset of web 1.0 and its evolution into web 2.0, digitization and the introduction of mobile applications, and most recently, generative AI and large language models. Recognizing the impact that these changes can have on your strategies, operating models, policies, and standards is critical, as is recognizing the relative maturity and risks associated with these changes.

Be a Trusted Advisor

As the CTO, you have been hired because of your expertise and experience. It is important to have a well-formed view on key technology decisions and, even more importantly, to demonstrate conviction in adverse situations. As a senior executive, there will be many factors to consider, and some situations will require compromise. You must lead with strength of conviction, stoic clarity, and unambiguous rationality to ensure that your perspective and views are well understood.

Will every one of your decisions land? No. But when they don't, the consequences you foresee must be well understood, and appropriate mitigations must be in place. Should these manifest, it is not a time for "I told you so." In fact, there is never a time for "I told you so." Collaboration and humility will lead to more weight and credence behind your opinion as a trusted advisor in the face of future challenges.

Velocity and Probabilistic Decision-Making

Earlier in my career, it seemed as though most decisions were somewhat deterministic: there was a right way and a wrong way. Success meant problem-solving, creating an efficient piece of code, or delivering an optimal solution. As I progressed further in my career, the likelihood of there being a single "right way" to achieve something diminished significantly. Suddenly, it became clearer and clearer that there were often many ways to solve a problem.

This led me to understand the importance of comprehending probabilistic decision-making. What does this mean? It means that there is a most appropriate decision based on the criteria that you used to "weight" your decision, *when* you are making the decision. There will be many "right ways." Your responsibility is to identify the "most appropriate" right way given what you know.

I have found that whenever there was a disagreement on the appropriate route forward, it was often not because one approach was right and one was wrong. Different people simply felt that different aspects of solving the problem were more important than others. Identifying and understanding these differences is an important part of convincing others of the merit of your decisions or to prompt *you* to reevaluate the right way forward.

I have also realized that it is often more important to make and communicate a decision with velocity, even with incomplete information, than it is to procrastinate, validate, and hold off on making a decision. When I have felt that I was *probably* right, that I *probably* had sufficient information, and that I had *probably* weighted the drivers appropriately, that was the right time to make the decision. As the CTO, decision velocity is important. Making adjustments later is far preferable to inactivity or indecision as a leader.

Stay Credible

As the *chief* technology officer, it is important to stay abreast of the broad technology landscape. You will not be able to maintain the level of technical skills that you had earlier in your career, but if you intend to be a credible leader, you must remain intellectually curious, inquisitive, and studious with regard to industry developments. I have always tried to hire and surround myself with other credible leaders who display this trait, as they are more likely to challenge my thinking and push my skills forward, ultimately resulting in better outcomes.

Nothing Takes a Week

When working on a problem or a deliverable, it is a red flag when the amount of time needed to complete an activity is "about a week." This is usually a sign of an incomplete understanding of what truly is required. And that's fine: not everything will be well understood at the moment it is requested. However, it is just as likely that there will still be missing information in a week's time, so compress the timescales and force the individual or team to face this fact as early as possible. It is likely that your input will be required, so where there is an imprecise timeline, push your teams to come back sooner so that you can iterate with them on the task at hand.

DELEGATION VERSUS DIRECTION

To be truly successful in your role, you will need a strong team that augments and complements your strengths. As such, there should be people far more capable than you to complete certain activities on your behalf. You must recognize this and delegate effectively.

But what is effective delegation? It is where you cease to be directive in your management of someone. You move from telling them *what to do* to telling them *what you want them to achieve*. Yes, you will still want them to operate within any constraints that you highlight and in line with your values, but the minutiae is theirs to manage. As a leader, exerting *influence* over *control* will ensure more sustainable outcomes and build trust and loyalty.

You must recognize, however, that there is a right and a wrong time to delegate to an individual. You and the person to whom you delegate must have confidence in achieving a successful resolution. I would like to share a simple but effective assessment that you can make to determine if it is appropriate to delegate.

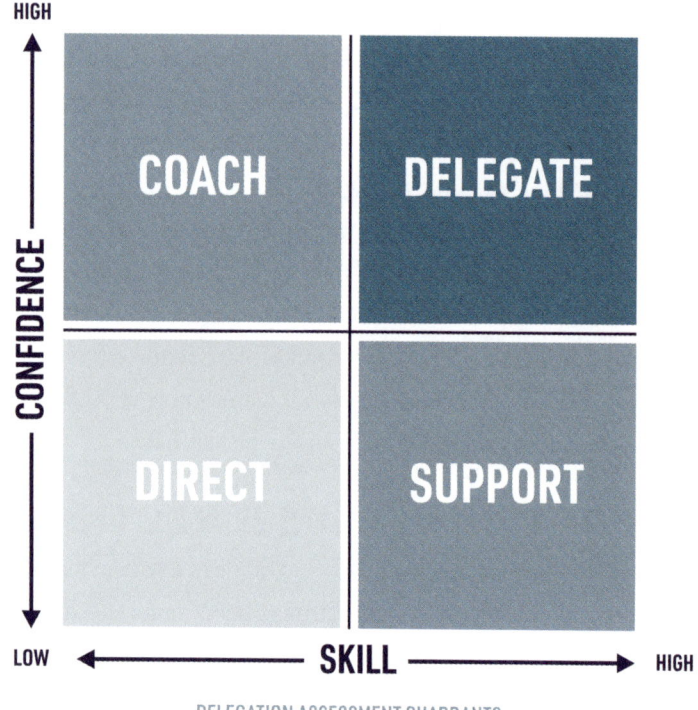

DELEGATION ASSESSMENT QUADRANTS

Consider two simple evaluations: the level of *Skill* that the individual has as it pertains to the task and the level of *Confidence* that they have in completing the task.

- Individuals with High Skill and High Confidence are those you should feel comfortable to **Delegate** to. They have the necessary skills to complete the task and are confident in their abilities to do so. They will drive the activity, and it is their responsibility to determine how best to engage and appropriately update you. You just need to validate the efficacy of their outcomes.

- Individuals with High Skill but Low Confidence are those you will need to **Support**. This should be comparatively low touch, as they have the right skills, but you need to support them to bolster their confidence in their ability to complete the task. You must be cognizant that they have the right skills, so it is important to listen, be supportive when they make good decisions, and leave them with the confidence to be confident next time.

- Individuals with Low Skill but High Confidence are those you will need to **Coach**. They believe they can complete the task, but they do not yet possess the necessary skills. You will need to more closely supervise their activity and define the mechanisms by which they engage and update you. They cannot be delegated to without close supervision. It can be useful to put these individuals into the team that you are delegating to so that they can assimilate the necessary skills through participation and observation.

- Individuals with Low Skills and Low Confidence are those you will need to **Direct**. These individuals are not yet ready to be delegated to and are not yet ready for this type of engagement.

Remember: Just because someone has previously been successful when delegated to does not necessarily mean that they will have the same confidence or appropriate skills the next time. This assessment is very dependent on the specifics of the activity and the individual's skills and confidence levels. As such, a new assessment should be made each time to ensure that your engagement and oversight are appropriate.

CULTURE SURPASSES PROCESS

When I moved from Oracle, a company with rigorous procedures in place to support all aspects of software design and engineering, to Goldman Sachs, a company that then had little cross-firm consistency in their engineering procedures, I remember feeling quite uncomfortable. What was the design process? How did we test software? How did we get things into production with consistent quality?

It was jarring to have lost the comfort that consistent processes and procedures provided. Every team seemed to have their own approach. But despite the absence of rigorous processes, things got done—really great things and quickly! This perplexed me. I challenged my manager: "How does anything get done here?" Her response: "Give it time. You'll figure it out." And I did.

It was soon apparent that there was a wide collective understanding of the firm's core principles and objectives. People were united in a common purpose. Though there was variety in the approach, people felt accountability for their projects and pride in their deliverables. That environment was liberating.

Why was Oracle one way and Goldman Sachs another? For Oracle, who had a distributed consultant workforce often working on-site at their clients' premises, it was important to establish consistent processes to ensure quality and unity. It was "the Oracle Way," and it worked for them. Clients could understand the process and review their expected deliverables.

At Goldman Sachs, the firm had very recently transitioned from being a private partnership to a public company. Their attitude was still very much about ensuring that it was profitable and that investments were beneficial and needed to be made. There were many occasions where, in a meeting, the following question would arise: "If it was *your* money we were spending, would you still do it?" This epitomized the attitudes that people had and the individual rigor they applied to everything they did.

As my career progressed, especially working in a highly regulated industry, it became clear that establishing consistent procedures and processes was a requirement, as was demonstrating that the right things were being done the right way to compliance officers and regulators. It was nonnegotiable.

What always stuck with me was the need to be conscious of developing and nurturing the right culture. I had to communicate our objectives and purpose and empower teams to operate with as much independence and autonomy as processes would allow. When they were successful, it was important to recognize it and celebrate it. Establishing the culture you want will be challenging, but as the technology leader, it is imperative that you set the tone and show the way.

CHAPTER 14

COMMUNICATION

*Communication works
for those who work at it.*
—JOHN POWELL

To be a successful CTO, it is not enough to establish appropriate strategies, policies, standards, and procedures. For true success, they must also be communicated effectively and then acted upon. You must consider who needs to simply be aware of them versus those who need to contribute to or comply with them. You must identify the most suitable forums and channels, as well as the format that will be most impactful.

There are many detailed books and classes regarding effective communication, so I will not try to replicate them. I can, however, provide some thoughts on what has been effective for me. First and foremost, I will reiterate the importance of the principle of *trust through transparency*, which should be pervasive through all aspects of your communication. Good, bad, or downright ugly, being transparent about successes or failures, accomplishments, and challenges will ensure that your integrity is maintained and ultimately help develop trust.

COMMUNICATION FORUMS

When trying to determine the most appropriate mechanism to convey something, the only truism that I have identified is what works for one person may not work for another. This is wholly understandable. We are all different in how we learn, engage, and absorb information. This means that you will need to establish a number of different channels and formats if you want to ensure that your key messages receive the greatest level of penetration and comprehension across your organization.

First and foremost, I would recommend establishing a regular *town hall forum* for all your staff. A quarterly cadence is frequent enough that you'll have something meaningful to share and is not too far apart that your staff feels a void in communication. It is worth reiterating that this should not be a forum where you talk at your staff. It is an opportunity for dialogue and interaction. Yes, you will want to ensure that you meet your communication objectives, but genuine interaction is imperative. I have not been averse to ensuring some questions are seeded into the audience, which ensures that someone breaks the ice, but credibility and trust will be lost if these are the only types of questions that you respond to. Be bold, be honest, and answer what you can in the moment. And if you don't have the answers at hand, commit to following up in a subsequent forum or channel. The benefits of being authentic significantly outweigh any feelings of inadequacy or fears of appearing fallible.

Depending on the scale of your organization, it may also be beneficial to host a smaller forum for your extended leadership team. Include anyone and everyone relevant, including those who may not be in your reporting line but nevertheless interact with technology. This is an opportunity to be even more candid and open and explicit on your objectives and expectations on them as your senior leaders.

Be receptive to suggestions as they are made. My communications team at Citigroup was wonderful at deriving innovative ways to ensure my messages were accessible and heard. We had the resources to create a weekly news show that distilled key updates and information for that week into a punchy ten-minute video. This was supported by abridged newsletters that did not try to convey every detail but encouraged the reader to follow links and read more. Remember, it may not be the best format for *you*—I was initially skeptical regarding the news show—but that does not mean it is not appropriate and appreciated by *others*.

ESTABLISHING CTO CHAMPIONS

Across the financial institutions that I have worked with and the technology industry as a whole, there is usually a cohort of very senior or expert resources at hand. They are sometimes called "fellows," "distinguished engineers," or other honorifics that identify them as people who have sustained technical achievements and shown exemplary engineering and technology leadership. They represent the preeminent distinction that they can achieve at your firm. Creating such a program is a powerful and effective way to ensure that your strategies and approach are validated and contributed to, especially where there are individuals with the appropriate skills. More importantly, it creates an impactful cohort of CTO champions who can help ensure the socialization and execution of your objectives.

This can be incredibly far-reaching and impactful, so it is of paramount importance to ensure rigor and credibility in the selection process when establishing your CTO champion program. Confirm that the candidates are prepared to engage and contribute with impact, and most importantly, ensure that once selected, the rest of the firm—and even the industry as a whole—will see this group as inspirational and aspirational role models.

I firmly believe that confirming this title should in no way be *directly* connected to any other corporate title or HR grade. The reality is that the most impactful and thoughtful leader in a particular technology, product, or methodology may simply be young and enthusiastic. Often, they have recently left an educational program in which they focused on relevant subject matter. Their expertise should be assessed in terms of their comprehension and the prowess they display in their identified topic. Of course, there will be an *indirect* correlation to their corporate title or HR grade—to have impact and credibility, they will also need to master the soft skills that can only develop over time, such as having impact without authority or persuasion and clarity in their presentations. These are traits of an impactful technical leader.

The main objectives for your CTO champions are as follows:

- To identify and empower exemplary technology leaders who will act as ambassadors for your objectives as CTO.

- To create a cohort of inspirational and aspirational role models who will inspire the rest of your technology staff and ideally the technology industry as a whole.

- To represent your firm in external events and forums—

whether working with clients, open-source projects, or technology events—demonstrating the technology prowess of your firm and potentially attracting like-minded talent.

- To be subject matter experts in their chosen topics, demonstrate sustained technical leadership, and shape strategies and develop competency at your firm through technical mentorship and collaboration.

- To ensure that the recognition and trust placed in them will help ensure that they are vested in your firm, improving the likelihood that they remain there.

CELEBRATE TECHNOLOGY

In terms of motivation, technologists are not so different from nontechnologists. Everyone tends to like upgraded corporate titles, flexible working arrangements, and pay increases. But there is one trait that seems to be a more prevalent motivator for technologists: public recognition of their solutions and achievements.

Without doubt, when a technologist has worked hard to create an innovative or impactful technology solution, they will nearly always relish an opportunity to share it with a *knowledgeable* audience. As the CTO, you have the opportunity to create events that can be designed to exhibit the impactful solutions and innovative technologies in use across your firm. These may be in-person events where individuals or teams present their offerings; "technology festivals" with manned booths where people can roam freely, explore areas of interest, and engage with teams; or awards ceremonies where submissions are judged, graded, and recognized.

You can establish a highly impactful forum through a relatively small investment of time and effort. Inspiration, idea sharing, and, if you are lucky, collaboration on products and services across your firm may all result. This is not unlike contributing to open-source projects—when a team or individual believes that their code or solutions will be viewed and judged by their peers, it has a tendency to promote rigor and quality. If you have already established a program for identifying your firm's CTO champions, you have a ready-made and willing group to drive the development of the forum. If they fail to have something to share across your firm, perhaps you selected the wrong cohort.

DIFFICULT CONVERSATIONS

As the CTO, there will be many times when you will inevitably have to complete a "difficult conversation," and in these situations, there is a natural tendency to avoid or postpone the conversation, which is understandable. Who wants to have unpleasant experiences? Surely if you wait long enough, the situation will resolve itself? Unfortunately not. Things left unsaid have a tendency to fester. As the avoided situation degrades, the conversation inevitably gets more onerous and difficult to complete. It is most wise to prepare in advance and have the conversation as soon as possible.

How exactly should you prepare? First, you must not let your own emotions creep into the conversation, although it is important to understand how the situation is making you feel. It is also important to truly understand the situation—what has *actually* happened, not what you *think* has happened, or how others may be *feeling* about what happened. Finally, before the conversation, you need to understand your intentions: What should happen as a direct result of this conversation?

One useful piece of advice a mentor once gave me applies

here: "If you do not feel physically sick when you are delivering the message, you are most probably softening the message, and it may not be heard." This may seem a tad harsh. But to be clear, the advice is not to be cruel or thoughtless in your delivery. You must simply be direct and follow through on your preparation. Ensure that you have been heard, and seek follow-through on what needs to happen as a result. It is important to actively listen, but remember, the intentions that you set out to achieve remain the ultimate goal.

CHAPTER 15

LAST WORDS

*If I had to live my life again,
I'd make the same mistakes, only sooner.*
—TALLULAH BANKHEAD

I would like to close this book by sharing a few things that do not fit cleanly into the other chapters but have nevertheless been instrumental in helping me as a CTO. Consider these my final top tips as you embark on your journey to becoming the preeminent technology leader at your firm.

LIVING IN "T"

The first is the ethos I have for life in general: you must live life at "T." For those unfamiliar with the term, "T" in financial services is the transaction or trade date on which a security is bought or sold. The settlement date follows—currently T+1—when, a day later, the order will be finalized, and the funds and security will be delivered. Many things happen before the transaction date, but the things that happen in T- ("T minus"), though not as rigorously tracked, are still consequential to the trade.

My ethos is that you have to live in the current moment—in "T"—and deal with the things that are happening right now. You will have invariably made mistakes in the past. You will have concerns or trepidation for things that may happen in the future. But you should not have any *regrets* for the things that *have happened* in the past or feel *fear* for the things that *may happen* in the future.

This outpouring of energy and emotion is fruitless. You cannot change what has happened already, and what may happen in the future is exactly that: a risk that has yet to materialize—feeling fear or concern merely acts to bring forward future stress for events that are yet to occur. If you spend an inordinate amount of time thinking outside of "T," it will only cause you to expend unnecessary energy and distract you from focusing on the things you should do right now.

I should reiterate the importance of *learning* from the past. Understanding where we have erred allows us to not repeat the same mistakes. Similarly, we can *plan* for the future to ensure that we are prepared to address the risks that may materialize. But both instances entail focusing on what we can actually do today.

I have found that focusing on the present allows me to concentrate on what must be addressed right now. This promotes a better understanding of whatever current situation or challenge that I must face. As a consequence, I feel far less stress. The things happening now need resolution, which invariably results in action, and in action you take control, which alleviates the stress and worry. I am no psychologist, but living in "T" works for me!

BE COMFORTABLE KNOWING WHAT YOU DON'T KNOW

This may seem like a simplistic piece of advice, but it always surprises me when I encounter other senior executives who seemingly do not comprehend when they do not know something as well as perhaps their role suggests they should. Invariably these individuals bluff, bully, or blab their way along rather than display perceived "weakness" or "shortcomings" in their understanding. As the chief technology officer, you may feel that you should be the font of all technology knowledge. Maybe you are a brilliant polymath who truly does *believe* that you know all, but the reality is that you will not always know *something* as well as required.

And that's okay. It is important to recognize this when the situation occurs. You are in this position because you have consistently demonstrated the ability to grow and adapt, and there is no doubt your prior experiences will ensure that you ask the right questions. Just stay credible and be prepared to learn from others. If you have built a strong team, be comfortable in asking for assistance and delegating activities to others who are better qualified to execute them. Ultimately it is more important to achieve a successful outcome than it is to appear infallible.

TRUST YOUR INSTINCTS

Throughout my career I have trusted and acted on my instincts. You may call it a gut feeling or a feeling in your bones, but in my experience, if things have not felt right, it was for good reason. Learning to trust your instincts and act on them is incredibly important. Use them to understand when you need to dig deep or push harder to reveal the evidence for why you feel as you do. But ultimately, never ignore these feelings; they should be a signal for you to act.

Those actions should initially be to seek additional information and details to validate and verify why your "spider sense" is tingling. This is important to complete for a number of reasons. As stated, you need to explore why things do not seem as they should, but you also need to ensure that your unconscious biases or feelings of fear of the unknown are not triggering this reaction.

There are a number of unconscious biases that we all have, including items such as *affinity bias*—where we tend to gravitate and trust people whom we are like—and *confirmation bias*—where we look for evidence that reinforces our existing beliefs—and many other such biases.[47] I encourage you to explore this topic, as almost certainly it will influence your instincts. How can it not? It is an unconscious bias, after all.

There may also be feelings of trepidation and fear when new or unknown items are presented to you. Completely understandable, but as I cover earlier in this book, we must embrace that fear and explore new innovations and developments. So your instincts are right, but they are indicating that you need to do further exploration. Once you've validated why your instincts are firing, act decisively and make your decision with velocity.

ACKNOWLEDGMENTS

There are many people whom I must thank for the support, encouragement, and kindness that they have shown, not just in helping me finish this book but also for those who have helped shape my career and understanding of technology leadership. First and foremost, I must thank Janet Tyler, who, back in the late 1980s as an operations leader at "the Prov," supported and encouraged me to complete the aptitude test that resulted in a career shift into technology. You need good luck and hard work to be successful, but you also need individuals to open doors and be advocates, and without Janet, I have no doubt my career would have gone in a completely different direction, so I am immensely grateful for her support at the time.

Over the years there has been a long list of subject matter experts whom I have had the great privilege of working with and learning from. I will no doubt miss many—my apologies—but it would be remiss to not extend my sincere thanks to Darren Witham, Richard Hegan, Nick Lloyd, Paul Wigham, Chuan Li, Moe Matar, Jonathan Meadows, Mike Rozycki, Chris Welland, Jody Spearing, Tony DiSanto, Carol Dewar, Pete Holden, Jim Carney, Martin Kennedy, Brandon Johnson, Clark Smith, Rhyddian Olds, Darren McHattie, Tim Hooley, Paul Uminski, and Steve McColl. Over the years, and at various firms that I have been privileged to have worked at, they have been collaborators, sounding boards, critics, and innovators. I can't thank you enough.

There have also been a number of great CIOs, CISOs, and other technology leaders from whom I have benefited through their coaching, support, and example, most notably Mike Whitaker, Mike Grimaldi, Al Tarasiuk, Andrew Porter, James Linnett, Stuart Riley, J.P. Rangaswami, Kirsty Galloway, Steve Strongin, Roy Joseph, Trevor Smith, and Peter Bright. These individuals, all very different in their approaches and skills, nevertheless collectively provided examples of exemplary leadership. Each has certainly helped me in ways that I am sure they will never fully appreciate.

I must extend my thanks to everyone at Amplify Publishing Group, especially Naren Aryal and Will Wolfslau, who showed great enthusiasm for this project from the outset, as well as CW Patrick and the whole creative team who have helped guide this fledgling author through the editorial and production processes with both patience and expertise.

Finally, I must thank my family and friends who have been part of this amazing journey with me, as without their support and encouragement along the way, it would have been so much less fun!

REFERENCES

1. The Investopedia Team, "Chief Technology Officer (CTO): Definition, How to Become One, Average Salary," Investopedia, updated May 21, 2024, https://www.investopedia.com/terms/c/chief-technology-officer.asp.

2. "Chief Technology Officer," Wikimedia Foundation, last edited November 1, 2024, 15:08, https://en.wikipedia.org/wiki/Chief_technology_officer.

3. "Eating Your Own Dog Food," Wikimedia Foundation, last edited October 3, 2024, 02:45, https://en.wikipedia.org/wiki/Eating_your_own_dog_food.

4. Gartner Information Technology Glossary, "Definition of Architecture," Gartner, accessed November 17, 2024, https://www.gartner.com/en/information-technology/glossary/architecture.

5. "TOGAF," The Open Group, accessed November 17, 2024, https://www.opengroup.org/togaf.

6. "The TOGAF Standard, 10th Edition," The Open Group, accessed November 17, 2024, https://publications.opengroup.org/standards/togaf/specifications/c220.

7. "About the Zachman Framework," Zachman International, accessed November 17, 2024, https://zachman-feac.com/zachman/about-the-zachman-framework.

8. Svyatoslav Kotusev, "Enterprise Architecture Frameworks: The Fad of the Century," BCS, July 28, 2016, https://www.bcs.org/articles-opinion-and-research/enterprise-architecture-frameworks-the-fad-of-the-century.

9. "Business Architecture Center of Excellence," Business Architecture Training and Services, accessed November 17, 2024, https://www.bacoe.org.

10. Chris Richardson, "What Are Microservices?," Microservices.io, accessed November 17, 2024, https://microservices.io.

11. Chris Richardson, "Pattern: Monolithic Architecture," Microservices.io, accessed November 17, 2024, https://microservices.io/patterns/monolithic.html.

12 Thomas H. Davenport, "What's Your Data Strategy?," Harvard Business Review, May–June 2017, https://hbr.org/2017/05/whats-your-data-strategy.

13 "Publications: Body of Knowledge," DAMA International, accessed November 17, 2024, https://www.dama.org/cpages/body-of-knowledge.

14 "Welcome to UML," Unified Modeling Language, accessed November 17, 2024, https://www.uml.org.

15 Apache Avro, "Documentation," Apache Software Foundation, last modified November 4, 2024, https://avro.apache.org/docs.

16 "What Is an Application Architecture?," Red Hat, March 9, 2020, https://www.redhat.com/en/topics/cloud-native-apps/what-is-an-application-architecture.

17 Gartner Information Technology Glossary, "Application Architecture," Gartner, accessed November 17, 2024, https://www.gartner.com/en/information-technology/glossary/application-architecture-aa.

18 Job Search Insights, "Software Architect vs. Application Architect: What Are the Differences?," CLIMB, October 5, 2022, https://climbtheladder.com/software-architect-vs-application-architect.

19 "Waltz," Fintech Open Source Foundation, accessed November 17, 2024, https://waltz.finos.org.

20 "FINOS," Fintech Open Source Foundation, accessed November 17, 2024, https://www.finos.org.

21 "What Is an Event-Driven Architecture?," Amazon Web Services, accessed November 17, 2024, https://aws.amazon.com/event-driven-architecture.

22 Azure Architecture Center, "N-Tier Architecture Style," Microsoft Learn, accessed November 17, 2024, https://learn.microsoft.com/en-us/azure/architecture/guide/architecture-styles/n-tier.

23 "What Is Microservices Architecture?," Google Cloud, accessed November 17, 2024, https://cloud.google.com/learn/what-is-microservices-architecture.

24 Nidhi Raj, "Minimum Viable Product (MVP): What It Is and How to Start," Atlassian, accessed November 17, 2024, https://www.atlassian.com/agile/product-management/minimum-viable-product.

25 Gio Lodi, "Accelerate Test-Driven Development with AI," GitHub, accessed November 17, 2024, https://github.com/readme/guides/github-copilot-automattic.

26 Kirill Fakhroutdinov, "UML Deployment Diagrams," uml-diagrams.org, accessed November 17, 2024, https://www.uml-diagrams.org/deployment-diagrams.html.

27 "The NIST Cybersecurity Framework (CSF) 2.0," NIST, February 26, 2024, https://nvlpubs.nist.gov/nistpubs/CSWP/NIST.CSWP.29.pdf.

28 Computer Security Resource Center, "Cybersecurity Framework," NIST, updated August 15, 2024, https://csrc.nist.gov/Projects/Cybersecurity-Framework/Filters#/csf/filters.

29 Pallavi Kalapatapu, "Top 15 Software Supply Chain Attacks: Case Studies," Outshift, last updated June 18, 2024, https://outshift.cisco.com/blog/top-10-supply-chain-attacks.

30 "Shared Responsibility Model," Amazon Web Services, accessed November 17, 2024, https://aws.amazon.com/compliance/shared-responsibility-model.

31 "MITRE ATT&CK," The MITRE Corporation, accessed November 17, 2024, https://attack.mitre.org.

32 "Terms of Use: MITRE ATT&CK," The MITRE Corporation, accessed November 17, 2024, https://attack.mitre.org/resources/legal-and-branding/terms-of-use.

33 "Blocking Public Access to Your Amazon S3 Storage," Amazon Web Services, accessed November 17, 2024, https://docs.aws.amazon.com/AmazonS3/latest/userguide/access-control-block-public-access.html.

34 Computer Security Resource Center, "Secure Software Development Framework," NIST, updated July 30, 2024, https://csrc.nist.gov/Projects/ssdf; Murugiah Souppaya, Karen Scarfone, and Donna Dodson, "Secure Software Development Framework (SSDF) Version 1.1: Recommendations for Mitigating the Risk of Software Vulnerabilities," NIST Special Publication 800-218, February 2022, https://nvlpubs.nist.gov/nistpubs/SpecialPublications/NIST.SP.800-218.pdf.

35 "Apache License, Version 2.0," The Apache Software Foundation, January 2004, https://www.apache.org/licenses/LICENSE-2.0.

36 Opensource.org, "The MIT License," Open Source Initiative, accessed November 17, 2024, https://opensource.org/license/mit.

37 Opensource.org, "Licenses," Open Source Initiative, accessed November 17, 2024, https://opensource.org/licenses.

38 "Jira: Issue and Project Tracking Software," Atlassian, accessed November 17, 2024, https://www.atlassian.com/software/jira.

39 Richard W. Puyt, Finn Birger Lie, and Celeste P. M. Wilderom, "The Origins of SWOT Analysis," *Long Range Planning* 56, no. 3 (June 2023): 102304, https://www.sciencedirect.com/science/article/pii/S0024630123000110.

40 CFI Team, "SMART Goals," Corporate Finance Institute, accessed November 17 2024, https://corporatefinanceinstitute.com/resources/management/smart-goal.

41 "American Time Use Survey," US Bureau of Labor Statistics, last modified June 19, 2019, https://www.bls.gov/tus/data/datafiles-0318.htm.

42 Amazon, "1997 Letter to Shareholders," Securities and Exchange Commission, accessed November 17, 2024, https://www.sec.gov/Archives/edgar/data/1018724/000119312518121161/d456916dex991.htm.

43 "In Pursuit of Digital Trust," ISACA, accessed November 17, 2024, https://www.isaca.org.

44 "COBIT: Control Objectives for Information Technologies," ISACA, accessed November 17 2024, https://www.isaca.org/resources/cobit.

45 Faisal I. Khan, Paul R. Amyotte, and Tanjin Amin, "2.2.1 Risk Matrix," in "Chapter One: Advanced Methods of Risk Assessment and Management: An Overview" of Methods in Chemical Process Safety 4 (2020): 1–34, https://www.sciencedirect.com/topics/engineering/risk-matrix#:~:text=The%20idea%20of%20a%20risk,becomes%20a%20purely%20qualitative%20approach.

46 "The IIA's Three Lines Model: An Update of the Three Lines of Defense," The Institute of Internal Auditors, July 2020, https://www.theiia.org/globalassets/documents/resources/the-iias-three-lines-model-an-update-of-the-three-lines-of-defense-july-2020/three-lines-model-updated-english.pdf.

47 Bailey Reiners, "Unconscious Bias: 18 Examples and How to Avoid Them in the Workplace," Built In, updated by Matthew Urwin, August 28, 2024, https://builtin.com/diversity-inclusion/unconscious-bias-examples.

ABOUT THE AUTHOR

James "Jim" Adams is a technologist who has immersed himself in the ever-evolving technology landscape since getting his first personal computer at age eleven. Professionally, he has worked for a number of prestigious firms, including Goldman Sachs, Citigroup, JP Morgan, and Deutsche Bank. At each he has had responsibilities for leading technology strategy, innovation, and operations. Driven by a belief that creativity is essential for technological transformation, James wrote *The Creative CTO* to share his insights on leading teams, fostering a culture of innovation, and thriving in a constantly evolving digital landscape. He is a keen artist, writer, and digital musician when not noodling with bits and bytes.